Rosary Family Prayer Book

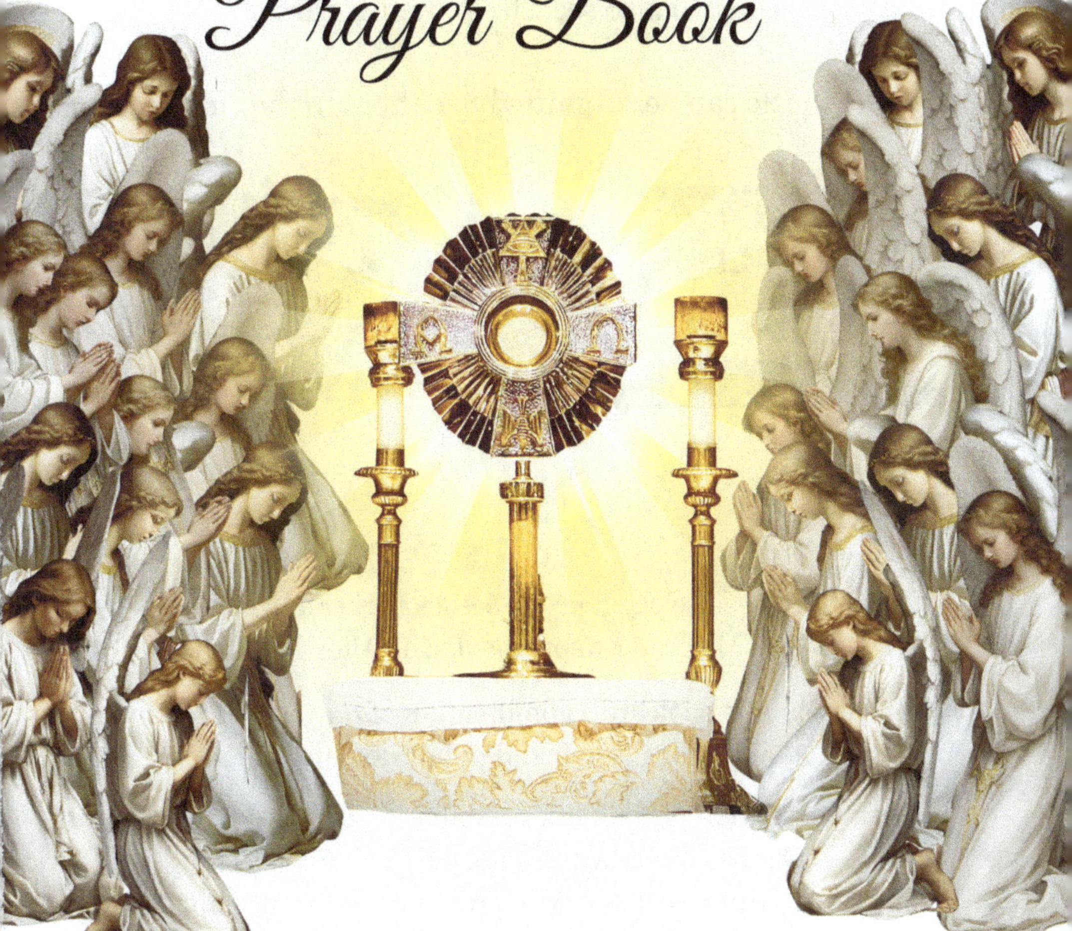

"We are the Rosary Family; we pray with each other and for each other."

PRAY TOGETHER LIVE

Join the Rosary Family to pray **LIVE** nightly on **Youtube at 8PM CST**

https://www.youtube.com/@frjamesparker777/streams

You can also search: Fr James Parker

Prayer requests can be submitted live through the chat section.

Prayers have been selected by Fr. James Parker and compiled by Marlene Knapp and Jackie Allor.

The prayers in this book are a combination of prayers of the Roman Catholic Church and public domain.

The artwork in this book is a combination of photography, Amber Knorr Art Studio, public domain, and AI-generated images. We have made every attempt to verify that these images are not copyrighted.

Amber Knorr Art can be purchased at https://www.amberknorrart.com/

www.littlewayspublishing.com

When We Pray

Matthew 18:19-20

Amen I say to you, if two of you agree on earth about anything for which they are to pray, it shall be granted to them by My Heavenly Father. For where two or three are gathered together in My name, there I am in the midst of them.

Psalm 66:19

But God did hear & listened to my voice in prayer.

Ephesians 3:12

In union with Christ and through our faith in Him we have the boldness to go into God's presence with all confidence.

1 John 5:14-15

We have courage in God's presence, because we are sure that He hears us if we ask Him for anything that is according to His will. He hears us whenever we ask Him; and since we know this is true, we know also that he gives us what we ask from Him.

1 Thessalonians 5:16-18

Be joyful always, pray at all times, be thankful in all circumstances. This is what God wants from you in your life in union with Christ Jesus. Do not restrain the Holy Spirit; do not despise inspired mesages. Put all things to the test: keep what is good and avoid every kind of evil.

BIG Intention Prayers

In this section, you can note **ONGOING prayers**, such as your children or grandchildren, for their faith, relationships, etc. Or intentions for job protection, family finances, end of atrocities in our country or world, faith to deepen, etc. In the back of the book is a section for other intentions.

Table of Contents

Rosary Family Format — 16
Opening Prayers
   1. The Sanctus — 17
   2. Holy Spirit Prayer — 17
   3. Short Prayer of Protection — 17
   4. The Miracle Prayer (adapted) — 18
   5. Spiritual Protection to Bind and Blind demons — 19
   6. Prayer of Authority — 20

Eucharistic Prayers
   7. Spiritual Communion — 21
   8. Angel of Fatima Prayer — 22
   9. The Unity Prayer — 22
   10. Anima Christi — 23
   11. St. Francis's Prayer Before the Crucifix — 23
   12. Offering of All Masses in the World — 23
   13. Prayer before the Blessed Sacrament — 23
   14. The Golden Arrow Prayer — 24

The Holy Rosary
Mysteries of the Holy Rosary
   15. O Sacrament Most Holy — 26
   16. Introductory Prayer to the Holy Rosary — 27
   17. Apostles Creed — 27
   18. Our Father/ Pater Noster — 28
   19. Hail Mary/ Ave Maria — 28
   20. Glory Be/ Doxologia Minor — 28
   21. Fatima Prayer/ Oratio Fatima — 29
   22. Hail Holy Queen — 29
   23. Concluding Prayer — 29
   24. St. Louis de Montfort Prayer to the Blessed Mother — 30

Daily Devotions
Our Lady
   25. Memorare — 32
   26. Take My Hand — 32
   27. Ancient Prayer to Mary — 32

28. Sacrifice Prayer	32
29. Act of Consecration to Mary	33
30. Short Prayer of Reparation to the Blessed Virgin Mary	33
31. O Domina Mea	33
32. Prayer of Entrustment to Our Lady	34
33. Sub Tuum Praesidium/ Your Protection	34

St. Joseph

34. Prayer to St. Joseph After the Rosary	35
35. St. Joseph Intercession Prayer	35
36. Ancient Prayer to St. Joseph	36

St. Padre Pio of Pietrelcina

37. Powerful Healing Prayer Attributed to St. Padre Pio	37
38. Spiritual Child of St. Padre Pio Prayer	38
39. Prayer for the Intercession of St. Padre Pio	38
40. Stay With Me	39
41. Prayer to Padre Pio for the Sick & Suffering	40

St. Therese of Lisieux

42. My Novena Rose Prayer	41
43. Shorter Novena to St. Therese of Lisieux	41
44. Memorare to the Little Flower of Jesus	42
45. Prayer to St. Therese, the Little Flower	42

Holy Angels

46. St. Michael	43
47. Guardian Angel Prayer	43
48. Angelic Protection	43
49. Gratitude for our Guardian Angel Prayer	43
50. Prayer to Our Guardian Angel	44
51. Send Your Guardian Angel to Mass	44
52. Prayer to St. Gabriel	45
53. Original Prayer to St. Michael	45
54. Prayer to St. Michael	45

Spiritual Protection

55. A Personal Prayer Against Evil	46
56. Renunciation Prayer-1	46
57. Renunciation Prayer-2	47

58. Prayer Against Every Evil	47
59. Psalm 91 Prayer	48
60. Commission of the Care of Soul and Body	49
61. Prayer of Blessing our Homes	49
62. Home Blessing	50
63. Mary, Bless This Home	51
64. I Consecrate My House	51
65. Litany of Blessing Home	52
66. Prayer for a Peaceful Home	53
67. Prayer to Mary for Liberation	53
68. Consecration of Exterior Goods to the Blessed Virgin Mary	54
69. Prayer of Command	55
70. Prayer for Breaking Ties	55
71. Prayer for Deliverance	56
72. Short Prayer Against Evil	56
73. Protection and Healing Prayer	57
74. Prayer for Deliverance	58
75. Prayer for Release from Ancestral Curses	59
76. St. Joseph Protection Prayer	59

Priestly Thursdays

77. Night Salutation and Prayer to Jesus in the Tabernacle	60
78. Chaplet of Reparation for Priests	61
79. Prayer for Priests through the Intercession	62

Prayers for Healing of Person & Family

- **Individual**

80. Bless Me, Heavenly Father	63
81. Holy Spirit Prayer	63
82. Come Holy Spirit	63
83. Powerful Prayer of Petition	64
84. Serenity Prayer	64
85. Learning Christ	65
86. Prayer in Union With Jesus	65
87. Prayer for Union With Jesus	66
88. A Healing Prayer	67

89. Short Healing Prayer	67
90. Prayer of St. Gertrude for Sleeplessness	68
91. Healing Prayer at Bedtime	68

- **Healing: Specific**

92. Prayer of St Gertrude the Great, Before Work	69
93. Holy Spirit Tension Prayer	69
94. Prayer During Difficult Times	69
95. Payer to Mary for Protection Against Danger	70
96. Prayer for Daily Challenges	70
97. Prayer for Enemies	71
98. Prayer to Redeem Lost Time	71
99. Prayer for Health	71
100. Prayer for Healing	72
101. Prayer of Charity	73
102. Prayer for Courage in Suffering	73
103. Gratitude in Suffering	74

- **Family**

104. Prayer for Marriages	75
105. Prayer for Healing My Family	75
106. Prayer for Broken Families	76
107. Prayer to St. Joseph, Protector	76
108. Prayer for Family Peace & Unity at Gatherings	77
109. Prayer for Protection Against Curses, Harm, and Accidents	78
110. Healing of the Family Tree	78
111. Release from Ancestral curses	78
112. Invocation Flame of Love	79
113. A Spiritual Communion to make for EACH Member of your Family	79
114. A Parent's Prayer	80
115. Miscarriage Prayer	81
116. Prayer for the Gift of Children/Grandchildren	82
117. Prayer for the Recovery of a Sick Person	82
118. Prayer for Those Suffering from Addiction	83
119. Prayer to Mother Mary for those Suffering with Cancer	83
120. The Purple Scapular Prayer	84

121. Healing Prayer Precious Blood of Jesus	84
122. Prayer for Peace	85
123. Prayer for Those in Their Last Agony	86
124. Prayer for the Recently Departed	86
125. Prayer to One's Guardian Angel for a Happy Death	87

Monthly Devotions & Novenas

First Wednesdays

126. Consecration to St. Joseph	89
127. Consecration to the Heart of St. Joseph	89
128. Holy Cloak of St. Joseph Novena	90

First Fridays

129. A Petition Prayer to the Sacred Heart of Jesus	97
130. Act of Reparation to the Sacred Heart of Jesus	97
131. Daily Act of Consecration to the Sacred Heart of Jesus	98
132. Within Thy Sacred Heart	99
133. Sacred Heart Novena Prayer	99
134. Prayer to the Sacred Heart of Jesus-1	100
135. Prayer to the Sacred Heart of Jesus-2	100
136. Invocations to the Sacred Heart	101

First Saturdays

137. Act of Reparation to the Immaculate Heart of Mary	102
138. Prayer to the Sacred Heart of Jesus & the Immaculate Heart of Mary-1	103
139. Prayer to the Sacred Heart of Jesus & the Immaculate Heart of Mary-2	104

January

140. Praise You Jesus	105
141. Veni, Creator Spiritus	106
142. Epiphany Home Blessing	107
143. Prayers for the Epiphany Home Blessing	107
144. Prayer to St. Sebastian	108
145. Novena to Our Lady Good Success	108
146. St. Don Bosco's Prayer to Mary	109

February

147. Feast of the Presentation Prayer	110

148. Consecration to the Flame of Holy Love	110
149. St. Blaise Intercession	110
150. Flame of Love Rosary	111
151. Novena to Our Lady of Lourdes	112
152. The Holy Face Novena	113
153. Prayer to the Holy Face of Jesus	113
154. Offering of the Holy Face of Our Lord Jesus Christ to God the Father	113

Lent
155. Prayer to Jesus Christ Crucified	114
156. Fatima Prayer- Reparation	114
157. Prayer to the Holy Face of Jesus- Reparation	115
158. Act of Consecration to the Holy Face of Jesus	116
159. Prayers of the Passion- Mother of Sorrows	117

March
160. Petition for St. Jospeh's Blessing	118
161. Act of Consecration to St. Joseph	118
162. Breastplate Prayer of St. Patrick	119
163. Good St. Joseph	119
164. Novena to St. Joseph	120

Divine Mercy Sunday
165. Our Lady of Mercy Prayer	121

April
166. Come Reign In Me	122
167. Novena to Our Lady of Good Counsel	123
168. Prayer to Our Lady of Good Counse6	124

May
169. Short Prayer of Reparation to the Virgin Mary	125
170. Novena to St. Dymphna	125
171. Prayer to St. Rita for Impossible Cases & Special Needs	126
172. Prayer to St. Joan of Arc	126

Pentecost
173. Consecration to the Holy Spirit	127
174. Daily Consecration to the Holy Spirit	127
175. Ablaze with the Fire of Your Spirit	127
176. Novena Holy Spirit	128

177. Prayer for the Seven Gifts of the Holy Spirit   129
178. Prayer to the Indwelling Most Holy Trinity   130
179. Act of Consecration to Our Lady of the Blessed Trinity   131

June
180. An Act of Consecration to the Sacred Heart of Jesus   132
181. Sacred Heart of Jesus   132
182. Sacred Heart of Jesus Consecration   132
183. Mother of Perpetual Help, For Graces & Salvation   133
184. Mother of Perpetual Help   133
185. Prayer to Sts. Peter and Paul for the Holy Catholic Church   134

July
186. Prayer for Calling on the Precious Blood of Our Lord   135
187. Prayer to the Precious Blood   135
188. Our Lady, The Immaculate Conception   136
189. Miracle Prayer to St. Benedict   136
190. St. Sharbel Intercession Prayer   136
191. Novena Prayer to Sts. Joachim & Ann   137
192. Novena to St. John Vianney   138
193. Prayer of St. Ignatius of Loyola   138

August
194. Immaculate Heart of Mary   139
195. Act of Entrusting a Soul to the Immaculate Heart of Mary   139
196. Our Lady, Queen of Angels   139
197. Prayer of St. John Vianney   140
198. Prayer to St. Philomena   140
199. Prayer to St. Maximilian Kolbe   140
200. Novena to Our Lady of the Assumption   141
201. Litany of Our Lady of Knock   142
202. St. Pius X Intercession Prayer   142
203. Invocation of the Entire Heavenly Court   143
204. Novena to Saint Monica   144
205. Our Lady of Częstochowa   144
206. Prayer of St. Augustine   145

September
207. Mother, Stand by me in my Last Hours   146
208. Prayer of St. Mother Teresa of Calcutta   146

209. Nativity of the Blessed Virgin Mary Prayer	147
210. Novena Prayer for the Intercession of St. Pio of Pietrelcina	147
211. Our Lady of Sorrows	148
212. The Seven Sorrows Rosary	148
213. Prayer to Mary, Undoer of Knots	151
214. Consecration Prayer to St. Michael	152
215. The Chaplet of St. Michael the Archangel	152
216. Act of Entrustment to St. Michael	153
217. Mary, Queen of the Angels	154
218. St. Michael Consecration Prayer	154
219. Prayer to Sts. Michael, Gabriel & Raphael	154
220. Miraculous Invocation to St. Therese of Lisieux	155

October

221. Consecration to the Holy Guardian Angel	156
222. Invocations of the Holy Guardian Angels	156
223. Peace Prayer of St. Francis of Assisi	157
224. Prayer for the Canonisation of Blessed Carlo Acutis	157
225. Novena for All Saints Day	158

November

226. O Gentlest Heart of Jesus	159
227. Prayer to the Sacred Heart for those in Purgatory	159
228. Prayer of Deliverance for the Poor Souls	160
229. Prayer of St. Gertrude the Great	160
230. Prayer of Blessed Miguel Pro.	160
231. Prayer to St. Joseph for a Soul in Purgatory	161
232. An Act of Mercy for Souls Suffering in Purgatory	161
233. Prayers for the Deceased for Every Day of the Week	162
234. Prayer to St. Cecilia	164
235. An Act of Thanksgiving	164
236. Act of Consecration to Our Lady of the Miraculous Medal	165
237. Prayer to Our Lady of Kibeho	166
238. Novena to the Immaculate Conception	167
239. Christ the King Prayer	168

December

240. St. Andrew Christmas Novena	169
241. Prayer of the Immaculate Conception	169

242. Prayer to Venerable Fulton Sheen 169
243. Prayer to the Virgin of Guadalupe 170
244. Prayer to St. Lucy 170
245. Traditional Prayer to Jesus in the Manger 171
246. Novena to the Infant Jesus of Prague 173
247. O Holy Infant, Jesus of Good Health 173
248. Novena to St. Elizabeth Ann Seton 174
249. Feast of the Holy Innocents 174
250. Prayer to the Holy Family 175
251. Intercession of Servant of God, Fr. John A. Hardon 176

Litanies/ Litany of…
252. Resignation to the Holy Will of God 178
253. The Sacred Heart of Jesus 180
254. The Precious Blood 182
255. Loreto 184
256. Immaculate Heart of Mary 187
257. Our Lady 189
258. St. Joseph 192
259. Supplications in honor of St. Joseph's hidden life with Jesus and Mary 194
260. St. Joseph for a Dying Person 196
261. Spiritual Warfare 197
262. The Saints 199
263. The Holy Angels 203
264. Supplication of the Holy Angels 206
265. St. Michael, the Archangel 209
266. Holy Souls in Purgatory 211
267. Healing for Families 213
268. The Dust 215
269. Humility 216
270. Waiting 217
271. Thanksgiving 218
272. As I Am Lord 220

Concluding Prayers
273. Surrender Prayers (Short & Long) 221

274. Fill in the Gap — 222
275. Fill in the Gap for deceased loved ones. — 222
276. Short Prayers — 223
277. Prayer for Daily Neglects — 223
278. A Night Prayer — 223
279. Healing Night Prayer — 223
280. Examination of Blessings — 224
281. Examination of Conscience — 225

Night Prayer

282. Penitential Act — 226
283. Salve Regina — 227
284. Night Blessing for a Good Sleep — 227
285. Final Blessing — 227
286. Salve Regina Song Sheet — 228

Rosary Family Format

Nightly Format:

Opening Prayers
-These prayers help us focus on God -

Holy Rosary
-There is a brief meditation before each decade, and some intentions will be read from the comments section; all comments will be included in a generic form of prayer. The last decade of the rosary is prayed in Latin.-

Daily Devotional Prayers
-These include Mary, St. Joseph, Holy Angels, Patrons Padre Pio, St. Therese of Lisieux, spiritual protection-

Prayers for the Healing of the Person & Family
-Prayers focusing for healing of person and family-

Monthly Devotional Prayers
-Prayers focusing on novenas or a devotion pertaining to that month/season.-

Litanies

Concluding Prayers
-Surrender prayers, examination of day, night prayer of Divine Office, final song & blessing-

Opening Prayers

1. The Sanctus

Holy, holy, holy, Lord, God of hosts. Heaven and earth are full of Your glory. Hosanna in the highest. Blessed is He who comes in the name of the Lord. Hosanna in the highest. Amen.

Sanctus, Sanctus, Sanctus Dominus Deus Sabaoth. Pleni sunt caeli et terra gloria tua. Hosanna in excelsis. Benedictus qui venit in nomine Domini. Hosanna in excelsis.

2. Holy Spirit Prayer

Come, Holy Ghost, fill the hearts of Thy faithful and enkindle in us the fire of Thy love. Send forth Thy Spirit, and they shall be created. And Thou shalt renew the face of the earth. O God, Who did instruct the hearts of the faithful by the light of the Holy Spirit, grant us by the gift of the same Spirit to have a right judgment in all things and ever to rejoice in His consolation. Through Christ our Lord. Amen.

3. Short Prayer of Protection

Lord Jesus Christ, we pray that Thou would cover us, our families, and all of our possessions with Thy love and Thy Most Precious Blood and surround all of us with Thy heavenly Angels, Saints, and the mantle of Our Blessed Mother. Thank you, Lord Jesus Christ. We ask this in Thy Most Holy Name. Amen.

Opening Prayers

4. The Miracle Prayer
(adapted)

Lord Jesus, I come before You (in this hour of prayer), just as I am. I am sorry for my sins, I repent of my sins, please forgive me.

In Your Name, I forgive all others for what they have done against me. I renounce Satan, the evil spirits, and all their works. I give You my entire self, Lord Jesus, now and forever. I invite You into my life, Jesus. I accept You as my Lord, God, and Savior. Heal me, change me, strengthen me in body, soul, and spirit. Come, Lord Jesus, cover me with Your Precious Blood and fill me with Your Holy Spirit. I love You, Lord Jesus. I praise You, Jesus. I thank You, Jesus. I shall follow You every day of my life. Amen.

Mary, My Mother, Queen of Peace, all the Angels and Saints, please help me. Amen.

Opening Prayers

5. Spiritual Protection to Bind and Blind demons

Most gracious Virgin Mary, thou who wouldst crush the head of the serpent, protect us from the vengeance of the evil one. We offer our prayers, supplications, sufferings, and good works to you so that you may purify them, sanctify them, and present them to your Son as a perfect offering. May this offering be given so that the demons that influence us (*could influence us or name the person*) do not know the source of the expulsion and blindness. Blind them so they know not our good works. Blind them so that they know not on whom to take vengeance. Blind them so that they may receive the just sentence for their works. Cover us with the Precious Blood of your Son so that we may enjoy the protection which flows from His Passion and Death. We ask this through the same Christ, Our Lord. Amen.

Opening Prayers

6. Prayer of Authority

Lord Jesus Christ, in Your Name, I take authority; I bind and silence all powers and forces that do not accept You as Lord and King, whether it be in the air, in the water, in the ground, in the netherworld, nature, and the spiritual world. I ask You to bind all demonic action and demonic communication. Lord, I seal this whole place, all of us here, and all our intentions in Your Precious Blood. I loosen the power of Your Precious Blood in our lives.

O Mary, Immaculate Queen, I humbly ask that you would surround us with your mantle of protection and crush Satan's power in our lives. St. Michael the Archangel, we ask you and all the Guardian Angels to protect us.

United with the Most Holy Trinity, Father, Son, and Holy Spirit **(+)**, I pray, Lord, that You would fill the rooms where we are praying, entire buildings, the homes, and the soil beneath the ground with Your Most Precious Blood and with the Holy Spirit leaving no space not filled with Your presence. We humbly thank You, Most Holy Trinity, for hearing and answering our prayers, leaving this entire area cleansed and healed from any evil presence or attachment. Lord Jesus Christ, I humbly pray that You would cover us, our families, our Rosary Family, and all of our possessions with Your love and Your Most Precious Blood. Surround us with Your heavenly Angels and Saints and the mantle of the Blessed Mother. We make this prayer, Lord Jesus, in Your Holy and saving Name. Amen.

Eucharistic Prayers

7. Spiritual Communion

My Jesus, I believe that You are present in the Most Holy Sacrament of the Altar. I love You above all things, and I desire to receive You into my soul. Since I cannot at this moment receive You sacramentally, come at least spiritually into my heart. I embrace You as if You were already there and unite myself wholly to You. Never permit me to be separated from You. Amen.

8. Angel of Fatima Prayer

My God, I believe, I adore, I hope, and I love You! I beg pardon for those who do not believe, do not adore, do not hope, and do not love You.

Most Holy Trinity, Father, Son, and Holy Spirit **(+)**, I adore You profoundly. I offer You the Most Precious Body, Blood, Soul, and Divinity of Jesus Christ, present in all the Tabernacles of the World in reparation for the outrages, sacrileges, and indifference by which He is offended. And, through the infinite merits of the Sacred Heart of Jesus and the Immaculate Heart of Mary, I beg of You the conversion of sinners. Amen.

9. The Unity Prayer

My adorable Jesus, may our feet journey together. May our hands gather in unity. May our hearts beat in unison. May our souls be in harmony. May our thoughts be as one. May our ears listen to the silence together. May our glances profoundly penetrate each other. May our lips pray together to gain mercy from the Eternal Father. Amen.

O Blessed Lady spread the effect of grace of thy flames of love over all humanity.

10. Anima Christi

Soul of Christ, sanctify me; Body of Christ, save me; Blood of Christ, inebriate me; Water from the side of Christ, wash me; Passion of Christ, strengthen me; O good Jesus, hear me; within Thy wounds, hide me; let me never be separated from Thee; from the evil one, deliver me; at the hour of my death, call me and bid me come to Thee, that with Thy Saints, I may praise Thee forever and ever. Amen.

11. St. Francis's Prayer Before the Crucifix

Most High, glorious God, enlighten the darkness of my heart and give me true faith, certain hope, perfect charity, sense, and knowledge, Lord, that I may carry out Your holy and true command. Amen.

12. Offering of All the Masses in the World

I unite myself with every Mass which at this time is being offered throughout the world. I place them in the hands of Mary, the Mediatrix of all Grace, that she may obtain by this presentation of the Blood of Christ to the Most Holy Trinity, the deliverance of souls from Purgatory, relief for the sick and dying, the conversion of sinners, and the perseverance of all the faithful. Amen.

13. Prayer before the Blessed Sacrament
by St. Francis of Assisi

We adore You, O Lord Jesus Christ, in this Church and all the Churches of the world, and we bless You because, by Your Holy Cross, You have redeemed the world. Amen.

Eucharistic Prayers

14. The Golden Arrow Prayer

May the most Holy, most Sacred, most Adorable, most Incomprehensible and Unutterable Name of God be always praised, blessed, loved, adored and glorified in Heaven, on earth, and under the earth, by all the creatures of God, and by the Sacred Heart of Our Lord Jesus Christ, in the Most Holy Sacrament of the Altar. Amen.

The Holy Rosary

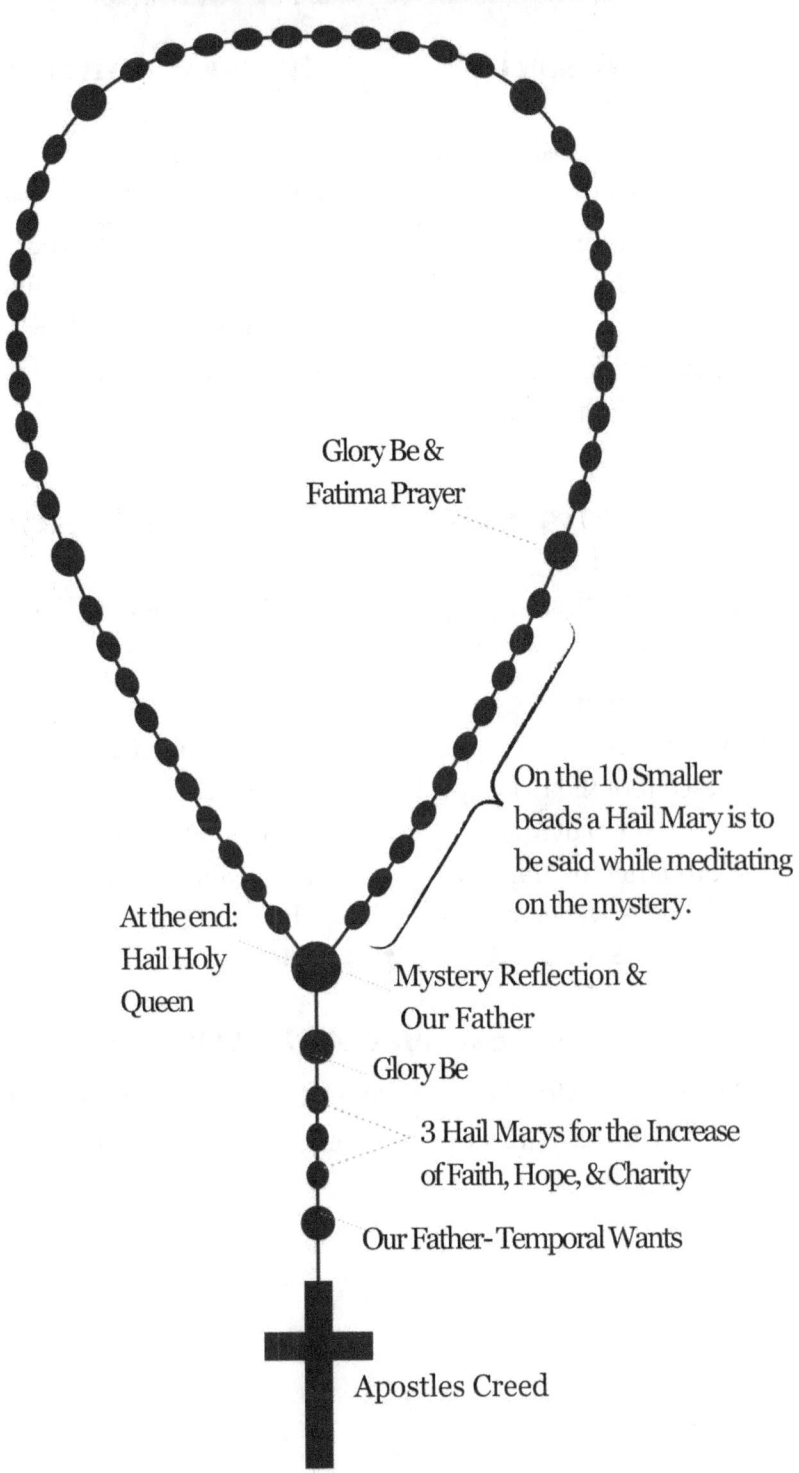

Mysteries of the Holy Rosary

Joyful Mysteries

Traditionally prayed on Mondays, Saturdays. During the season of Advent, on Sundays.

The Annunciation
The Visitation
The Nativity
The Presentation in the Temple
The Finding in the Temple

Sorrowful Mysteries

Traditionally prayed on Tuesdays, Fridays. During the season of Lent, on Sundays.

The Agony in the Garden
The Scourging at the Pillar
The Crowing with Thorns
The Carrying of the Cross
The Crucifixion

Glorious Mysteries

Traditionally prayed on Wednesdays. Outside the seasons of Advent and Lent, on Sundays.

The Resurrection
The Ascension
The Descent of the Holy Spirit
The Assumption of Mary
The Coronation of Mary as
  Queen of Heaven and Earth

Luminous Mysteries

Traditionally prayed on Thursdays.

The Baptism of Jesus
The Wedding Feast at Cana
The Proclamation of the
  Kingdom of God
The Transfiguration
The Institution of the Eucharist

---

15. O Sacrament Most Holy

O Sacrament Most Holy, O Sacrament Divine, all praise and thanksgiving be every moment Thine. Amen.

The Holy Rosary

16. Introductory Prayer to the Holy Rosary
by St. Louis de Montfort

I unite with all the Saints in heaven, with all the just on earth, and with all the faithful here present. I unite with Thee, my Jesus, in order to praise Thy holy Mother worthily and to praise Thee in her and through her. I renounce all the distractions that may come to me while I am praying this Rosary. I desire to say it with attention and devotion as if it were to be the last of my life.

O Blessed Virgin Mary, we offer you this Creed to honor the faith you had upon earth and to ask you to permit us to share in that same faith. O Lord, we offer Thee this, Our Father, to adore Thee in Thy oneness and to recognize Thee as the first cause and the last end of all things.

Most Holy Trinity, we offer Thee these three Hail Marys to thank Thee for all the graces which Thou hast given to Mary and which Thou hast given to us through her intercession. Amen.

17. Apostles Creed

I believe in God, the Father Almighty, Creator of Heaven and earth. I believe in Jesus Christ, His only Son, our Lord, who was conceived by the Holy Spirit and born of the Virgin Mary. He suffered under Pontius Pilate, was crucified, died, and was buried; He descended into hell. The third day, He rose again from the dead. He ascended to heaven and is seated at the right hand of God the Father Almighty. From there, he will come to judge the living and the dead. I believe in the Holy Spirit, the Holy Catholic Church, the Communion of Saints, the forgiveness of sins, the resurrection of the body, and life everlasting. Amen.

18. Our Father/ Pater Noster

Our Father, Who art in Heaven, Hallowed be Thy Name. Thy Kingdom come. Thy Will be done, on earth as it is in Heaven. Give us this day our daily bread. And forgive us our trespasses, as we forgive those who trespass against us. And lead us not into temptation, but deliver us from evil. Amen.

Pater noster, qui es in cælis, sanctificétur nomen tuum. Advéniat regnum tuum. Fiat volúntas tua, sicut in cælo, et in terra. Panem nostrum quotidiánum da nobis hódie, et dimítte nobis débita nostra sicut et nos dimíttimus debitóribus nostris. Et ne nos indúcas in tentatiónem, sed líbera nos a malo. Amen.

19. Hail Mary/ Ave Maria

Hail, Mary, full of grace, the Lord is with thee. Blessed art thou amongst women and blessed is the fruit of thy womb, Jesus. Holy Mary, Mother of God, pray for us sinners, now and at the hour of our death. Amen.

Ave María, grátia plena, Dóminus tecum; benedícta tu in muliéribus, et benedíctus fructus ventris tui, Iesus. Sancta María, Mater Dei, ora pro nobis peccatóribus, nunc, et in hora mortis nostræ. Amen.

20. Glory Be/ Doxologia Minor

Glory be to the Father, and to the Son, and to the Holy Spirit. As it was in the beginning, is now, and ever shall be, world without end. Amen.

Glória Patri, et Fílio, et Spirítui Sancto. Sicut erat in princípio, et nunc, et semper, et in sæcula sæculórum. Amen

21. Fatima Prayer/ Oratio Fatima

O my Jesus, forgive us our sins, save us from the fires of hell, lead all souls to heaven, especially those who are in most need of Thy mercy. Amen.

O Mi Jesu, dimitte nobis débita nostra, salva nos ab igne inferni; perduc in caelum omnes ánimas, praesertim eas, quae misericórdiae tuae máxime indigent. Amen.

22. Hail Holy Queen

Hail, Holy Queen, Mother of Mercy, our life, our sweetness and our hope. To you do we cry, poor banished children of Eve. To you do we send up our sighs, mourning and weeping in this valley of tears; turn then, most gracious advocate, your eyes of mercy toward us, and after this exile, show unto us the blessed fruit of thy womb, Jesus.

O clement, O loving, O sweet Virgin Mary. Pray for us, O Holy Mother of God, that we be made worthy of the promises of Christ.

23. Concluding Prayer

Let us pray: O God, whose Only Begotten Son, by His life, Death, and Resurrection, has purchased for us the rewards of eternal life, grant, we beseech thee, that while meditating on these mysteries of the Most Holy Rosary of the Blessed Virgin Mary, we may imitate what they contain and obtain what they promise, through the same Christ our Lord. Amen.

24. St. Louis de Montfort Prayer to the Blessed Mother

Hail Mary, beloved Daughter of the Eternal Father, admirable Mother of the Son, faithful Spouse of the Holy Spirit, august Temple of the most Holy Trinity! Hail, Sovereign Princess, to whom all owe subjection in Heaven and on earth! Hail, sure Refuge of Sinners, Our Lady of Mercy, who hast never refused any request. All sinful though I am, I cast myself at thy feet and beseech thee to obtain from Jesus, thy beloved Son, contrition and pardon for all my sins, as well as the gift of Divine Wisdom. I consecrate myself entirely to thee with all that I have. I choose thee today for my Mother and Mistress. Treat me, then, as the least of thy children and the most obedient of thy servants. Listen, my Princess, listen to the sighs of a heart that desires to love and serve thee faithfully. Let it never be said that of all those who have had recourse to thee, I was the first to be abandoned. O my hope, O my life, O my faithful and Immaculate Virgin Mary, defend me, nourish me, hear me, teach me, and save me. Amen.

With these beads, I bind our Rosary Family to Mary's beautiful Immaculate Heart. O Blessed Virgin Mary, I entrust and I consecrate our Rosary Family to the Immaculate Heart; please intercede on our behalf for all of our petitions, those in the silence of our heart & those on our screen.

Daily Devotions

15 Promises

of the Rosary

Promises 1-5

1. Those who faithfully serve me by the recitation of the Rosary shall receive signal graces.
2. I promise my special protection and the greatest graces to all those who shall recite the Rosary.
3. The Rosary shall be a powerful armor against hell. It will destroy vice, decrease sin, and defeat heresies.
4. The recitation of the Rosary will cause virtue and good works to flourish. It will obtain for souls the abundant mercy of God. It will withdraw the hearts of men from the love of the world and its vanities and will lift them to the desire of eternal things. Oh, that souls would sanctify themselves by this means.
5. The soul which recommends itself to me by the recitation of the Rosary shall not perish.

Our Lady

25. Memorare

Remember, O most gracious Virgin Mary, that never was it known that anyone who fled to thy protection, implored thy help, or sought thine intercession was left unaided. Inspired by this confidence, I fly unto thee, O Virgin of virgins, my mother; to thee do I come, before thee I stand, sinful and sorrowful. O Mother of the Word Incarnate, despise not my petitions, but in thy mercy hear and answer me. Amen.

26. Take My Hand

Take my hand, O Blessed Mother. Hold me firmly 'lest I fall. If I'm nervous while I'm walking, quickly heed my humble call. Guide me over every crossing. Watch me when I'm on the stairs. Let me know you're beside me. Listen to my fervent prayers. Bring me to my destination. Keep me safe along the way. Bless my every undertaking and my duties for the day. When the evening draws upon me, I do not fear to be alone. Once again, O Blessed Mother, take my hand and lead me home. Amen.

27. Ancient Prayer to Mary

We turn to you for protection, Holy Mother of God. Listen to our prayers, and help us in our needs. Save us from every danger, O glorious Blessed Virgin. Amen.

28. Sacrifice Prayer

O My Jesus, I offer this for love of Thee, for the conversion of sinners, and in reparation for the sins committed against the Immaculate Heart of Mary. Amen.

29. Act of Consecration to Mary

O Mary, Immaculate Queen, glorious Queen of the Universe, most powerful Virgin, merciful Mother of a merciful God and refuge of sinners, we consecrate ourselves to thy Royal and Immaculate Heart. It is through thee that Jesus Christ our King has come into the world to save it. It is also through thee that He is to reign over the world. In order to obtain this great benefit for ourselves and all mankind, we come to thy feet to consecrate to thee our persons, our lives, all that we are, all that we have, and all that we love. Keep us, enlighten us, dispose of us, reign over us. May all hearts and all homes willingly proclaim thee as their Immaculate Queen. Amen.

30. Short Prayer of Reparation to the Blessed Virgin Mary

O Mary, bless this house, where thy name is ever held in benediction. All glory to Mary ever Immaculate, ever Virgin, blessed among women, the Mother of our Lord Jesus Christ, Queen of Paradise. Amen.

Cover this house with the mantle of your protection, Mother of Mercy!

31. O Domina Mea
by St. Aloysius Gonzaga

O Holy Mary, my mistress, into your blessed trust and special custody and into the grasp of your mercy, I commend my soul and body this day, every day, and in the hour of my death. To you, I commit, all my anxieties and miseries, my life and the end of my life, that by your most holy intercession and by your merits, all my actions may be directed and disposed according to your will and that of your Son. Amen

32. Prayer of Entrustment to Our Lady

My Queen and my Mother, I give myself entirely to you, and to show my devotion to you, I consecrate to you this day my eyes, my ears, my mouth, my heart, my whole being without reserve. Wherefore, good mother, as I am your own, keep me, guard me, as your property and possession.

My Queen! My Mother! Remember, I am yours. Keep me, guard me as your property. O Mary Immaculate Virgin! Offer to the Heavenly Father the Precious Blood of your Son, Jesus Christ, that by its power, a mortal sin may be prevented in the world. Amen.

33. Sub Tuum Praesidium/Your Protection

3rd Century Prayer to Mary

We fly to thy protection, O Holy Mother of God, despise not our petitions in our necessities, but always deliver us from all dangers, O glorious and Blessed Virgin. Amen.

St. Joseph

34. Prayer to St. Joseph After the Rosary
Especially in the month of October

To you, O blessed Joseph, we have recourse in our affliction. And having implored the help of your thrice-holy Spouse, we now, with hearts filled with confidence, earnestly beg you to take us also under your protection. By that charity with which you were united to the Immaculate Virgin Mother of God, and by that fatherly love with which you cherished the Child Jesus, we beseech you, and we humbly pray that you will look down graciously upon that inheritance which Jesus Christ purchased by His Blood, and will help us in our need by your power and strength.

Defend, O most watchful guardian of the Holy Family, the chosen offspring of Jesus Christ. Keep from us, O most loving Father, all blight of error and corruption. Aid us from on high, most valiant defender in this conflict with the powers of darkness. As you once rescued the Child Jesus from deadly peril, so now defend God's Holy Church from the snares of the enemy and from all adversity. Shield us ever under your patronage, that, following your example and strengthened by your help, we may live a holy life, die a happy death, and attain to everlasting bliss in Heaven. Amen.

35. St. Joseph Intercession Prayer

O St. Joseph, Virgin father of Jesus, most pure spouse of the Virgin Mary, pray for us daily to the Son of God, that armed with the weapons of His Grace, we may fight as we ought in life and be crowned by Him in death. Amen.

36. Ancient Prayer To St. Joseph

O St Joseph, whose protection is so great, so strong, so prompt before the throne of God, I place in you all my interests and desires. O St Joseph, do assist me by your powerful intercession and obtain for me, from your Divine Son, all spiritual blessings through Jesus Christ, Our Lord, so that, having engaged here below your heavenly power, I may offer you my thanksgiving and homage to the most loving Father.

O St Joseph, I never weary contemplating you and Jesus asleep in your arms. I dare not approach while He reposes near your heart. Press Him in my name, and kiss His fine head for me, and ask Him to return the kiss when I draw my dying breath. St Joseph, Patron of departing souls, pray for me. Amen.

St. Padre Pio of Pietrelcina

37. Powerful Healing Prayer attributed to St. Padre Pio

Heavenly Father, I thank You for loving me. I thank You for sending Your Son, Our Lord Jesus Christ, to the world to save and to set me free. I trust in Your power and grace that sustain and restore me.

Loving Father, touch me now with Your healing hands, for I believe that Your will is for me to be well in mind, body, soul, and spirit. Cover me with the Most Precious Blood of Your Son, our Lord, Jesus Christ, from the top of my head to the soles of my feet.

Cast out anything that should not be in me. Root out any unhealthy and abnormal cells. Open any blocked arteries or veins and rebuild and replenish any damaged areas. Remove all inflammation and cleanse any infection by the power of Jesus' Precious Blood.

Let the fire of Your healing love pass through my entire body to heal and make new any diseased areas so that my body will function the way You created it to function. Touch my mind and emotion, even the deepest recesses of my heart.

Saturate my entire being with Your presence, love, joy, and peace, and draw me ever closer to You every moment of my life. And Father, fill me with Your Holy Spirit and empower me to do your works so that my life will bring glory and honor to Your Holy Name. I ask this in the Name of the Lord Jesus Christ. Amen.

38. Spiritual Child of St. Padre Pio Prayer

O St. Padre Pio, please be a spiritual father to our Rosary Family. Help us to always pray, hope, and not to worry but to trust in Jesus. Help us to have a greater love for our Eucharistic Lord, His Cross, and the Blessed Virgin Mary and her rosary.

O Saint Padre Pio, holy bearer of the Wounds of Christ, accept us this day as your spiritual sons and daughters and keep us always on the narrow path by your intercession. And do thou, O our Spiritual Father, stay there at the Gates of Heaven until all your spiritual children have entered through, even including us. Through Christ our Lord, Amen.

39. Prayer for the Intercession of St. Padre Pio of Pietrelcina

O God, You gave Saint Pio of Pietrelcina, Capuchin Priest, the great privilege of participating in a unique way in the Passion of Your Son, grant me through his intercession the grace of (*mention here*), which I ardently desire; and, above all, grant me the grace of living in conformity with the death of Jesus, to arrive at the glory of the resurrection.

Glory be to the Father ... (3x).

40. Stay With Me
By St. Padre Pio

Stay with me, Lord, for it is necessary to have You present so that I do not forget You. You know how easily I abandon You.

Stay with me, Lord, because I am weak, and I need Your strength that I may not fall so often.

Stay with me, Lord, for You are my life, and without You I am without fervor.

Stay with me, Lord, for You are my Light, and without You, I am in darkness.

Stay with me, Lord, to show me Your will.

Stay with me, Lord, so that I hear Your voice and follow You.

Stay with me, Lord, for I desire to love You very much and always be in Your company.

Stay with me, Lord, if You wish me to be faithful to You.

Stay with me, Lord; as poor as my soul is, I want it to be a place of consolation for You, a nest of Love.

Stay with me, Jesus, for it is getting late, and the day is coming to a close, and life passes, death, judgment, and eternity approaches. It is necessary to renew my strength so that I will not stop along the way, and for that, I need You. It is getting late, and death approaches; I fear the darkness, the temptations, the dryness, the cross, the sorrows. O, how I need You, my Jesus, in this night of exile!

Stay with me tonight, Jesus; in life with all its dangers, I need You. Let me recognize You as Your disciples did at the breaking of the bread so that the Eucharistic Communion be the Light which disperses the darkness, the force which sustains me, the unique joy of my heart.

Stay with me, Lord, because at the hour of my death, I want to remain united to You, if not by Communion, at least by grace and Love.

Stay with me, Lord, for it is You alone I look for, Your Love, Your Grace, Your Will, Your Heart, Your Spirit, because I love You and ask no other reward but to love You more and more. With a firm love, I will love You with all my heart while on earth and continue to love You perfectly during all eternity. Amen.

Relic of St. Pio's Crust of the Wounds

Relic of St. Pio's Mantle

41. Prayer to Padre Pio for the Sick & Suffering

O Glorious St. Pio, patron of those who are in need of healing, I call upon you and seek your help. Please intercede for all those who are in need of spiritual, emotional, or physical healing.

Obtain for them comfort during their sufferings, strength when they feel weary, hope when they feel discouraged, and joy when they are down-hearted. Help them know the peace of Jesus and the certainty of His victory in their suffering through Christ Our Lord. Amen.

 ## St. Therese of Lisieux

42. My Novena Rose Prayer

O Little Therese of the Child Jesus, please pick for me a rose from the heavenly garden and send it to me as a message of love. O Little Flower of Jesus, ask God to grant the favors I now place with confidence into your hands, *for all the petitions here tonight, for all those praying with us later, for my brother priest on the sidelines.*

O St Therese, help me to always believe, as you did, in God's great love for me so I may imitate your "Little Way" with love each day. Help us to practice your "little way" of joyful, humble, confident trust in the Father's love for us. Amen.

43. Shorter Novena to St. Therese of Lisieux

O Little Therese of the Child Jesus, please pick for me a rose from the heavenly gardens and send it to me as a message of love. St. Therese, help me to always believe as you did, in God's great love for me, so that I might imitate your "Little Way" each day. Amen.

44. Memorare to the Little Flower of Jesus

Remember, O most gracious St. Therese, your promise of never leaving any request made to you without an answer and of coming down to earth to do good. Full of confidence in your power with the Sacred Heart of Jesus, we implore your intercession in our need and beg of you to obtain the Rose we so urgently request if such be God's Holy Will. Amen.

45. Prayer to St. Therese, the Little Flower

St. Therese, the Little Flower, please pick a rose for me from the heavenly garden of our Divine Savior and send it to me as a message of love. Since you promised to spend your heaven doing good on earth, please look favorably upon my petitions. Speedily recommend them to the Sacred Heart of Jesus and beg Him to grant my requests *(mention here)*. If this favor is granted to me, I will seek to imitate you more and to be ever more loving and charitable, especially towards God's little and least ones. St. Therese, pray for me and for all my loved ones. Amen.

Holy Angels

46. St. Michael

Saint Michael the Archangel, defend us in battle. Be our protection against the wickedness and snares of the devil; May God rebuke him, we humbly pray; And do thou, O Prince of the Heavenly Host, by the power of God, thrust into hell Satan and all evil spirits who wander through the world seeking the ruin of souls. Amen.

47. Guardian Angel Prayer

Angel of God, my guardian dear, to whom God's love commits me here, ever this day, be at my side, to light and guard, to rule and guide. Amen.

48. Angelic Protection

Lord, Holy Father, Almighty, and Eternal God, hear us and deign to send Your holy Angels to watch over everyone who comes to this house and to protect, guard, defend, and look after them. Amen.

49. Gratitude for Our Guardian Angel Prayer

My God, I thank You for all the graces You have given to my, dear Angel. My God, I thank You for giving me this great Angel to be my brother and friend. My dear Angel, I thank you a thousand times for the countless favors you have done for me, for the countless times you have saved me from evils and dangers. My Angel, I love you with all my heart. Make me feel your presence at my side. Amen.

50. Prayer to Our Guardian Angel

O most faithful companion, appointed by our Heavenly Father to be my guardian, I thank you for your protection, kindness, caring, and love and for the benefits you have obtained for me. O holy Angel, always protect me throughout the day and night while I sleep. Comfort me when I am sad. Avert all dangers and evil that threaten and warn me of those to come. Protect and keep my and my family's homes free from danger and evil at all times. Always turn me away from sin and inspire me to do good. Encourage me to do penance when I fall and to reconcile me to God. Do not leave me, heavenly guide. Protect my heart, mind, and body at all times. Protect me in adversity, protect me in success, always protect me in danger, always protect me and always keep any and all evil far, far away from me, and always protect me from all temptations so that I do not fall. Offer up in the sight of the Divine Majesty all my prayers and petitions and all my charitable works, help me persevere in my faith, and always keep me in grace and holiness until I enter into everlasting life. Amen.

51. Send Your Guardian Angel to Mass

O Guardian Angel at my side, go to the church for me. Kneel in my place at Holy Mass, where I desire to be. At offertory, in my stead, take all I am and own and place it upon the altar throne as a sacrifice. At Holy Consecration's bell, adore with seraph's love, My Jesus hidden in the Host, come down from Heaven above.

Then pray for those I dearly love and those who cause me grief, that Jesus' Blood may cleanse all hearts and suffering souls relieve. And when the priest Communion takes, oh, bring my Lord to me, that His sweet Heart may rest on mine, and I, His temple be. Pray that this Sacrifice Divine, may mankind's sins efface; Then bring me Jesus' blessing home, the pledge of every grace. Amen.

52. Prayer to St. Gabriel

Glorious Archangel St. Gabriel, the powerful messenger of God, You announced to Mary the birth of our Savior and, in doing so, brought hope to the world. We pray that you would intercede for us with God the Father. Through your intercession, may we receive the strength of mind and heart to fulfill our mission here on earth so that we may one day praise the Heavenly Father with all of the Angels and Saints in Heaven. Amen.

53. Original Prayer to St. Michael

O God, the Father of our Lord Jesus Christ, we call upon Thy Holy Name, and as supplicants, we implore Thy clemency, that by the intercession of Mary, ever Virgin Immaculate and our Mother, and of the glorious St. Michael the Archangel, Thou wouldst deign to help us against Satan and all the other unclean spirits who wander about the world for the injury of the human race and the ruin of souls. Amen.

54. Prayer to St. Michael

Saint Michael, the Archangel, Glorious Prince, chief, and champion of the heavenly hosts; guardian of the souls of men, conqueror of the rebel Angels! How glorious art thou, in thy heaven-made armor. We love thee, dear Prince of Heaven! We, thy happy clients, yearn to enjoy thy special protection. Obtain for us from God a share of thy sturdy courage; pray that we may have a strong and tender love for our Redeemer and, in every danger or temptation, be invincible against the enemy of our souls. O standard-bearer of our salvation! Be with us in our last moments, and when our souls quit this earthly exile, carry them safely to the judgment seat of Christ, and may Our Lord and Master bid thee bear us speedily to the kingdom of eternal bliss. Teach us ever to repeat the sublime cry: "Who is like unto God?" Amen.

Spiritual Protection

55. A Personal Prayer Against Evil

Lord, Almighty, Merciful, and Omnipotent God, Father, Son, and Holy Spirit (+), drive out from me all influence of evil spirits.

Father, in the Name of Jesus Christ, I plead You to break any chain that the devil has on me. Pour upon me the Most Precious Blood of Your son. May His Immaculate and Redeeming Blood break all bonds of my body or mind. I ask You this through the intercession of the Blessed Virgin Mary.

Archangel St. Michael, intercede and come to my help.

In the Name of Jesus, I command all demons that could have any influence over me to leave me forever. By His scourging, His Crown of Thorns, His Cross, by His Blood and Resurrection, I command all evil spirits to leave me. By the true God, by the Holy God, by God who can do all, in the Name of Jesus, my Savior and Lord, leave me. Amen.

56. Renunciation Prayer-1

In the Name of Jesus Christ, by the power of His Precious Blood, may any power or hold the devil has over me be utterly destroyed. May the Blessed Virgin Mary, St. Michael with all the Angels and Saints be with me to protect me. Amen.

Daily Devotion: Spiritual Protection

57. Renunciation Prayer-2

In the Name of Jesus Christ, by the power of my Baptism, I bind and chain (*mention here*), and I send it to the foot of the Holy Cross. Amen.

58. Prayer Against Every Evil

Spirit of our God, Father, Son, and Holy Spirit (+), Most Holy Trinity, Immaculate Virgin Mary, Angels, Archangels, and Saints of Heaven descend upon me.

Please purify me, Lord, mold me, fill me with yourself, use me. Banish from me all the forces of evil, destroy them, vanquish them so that I can be healthy and do good deeds.

Banish from me all spells, witchcraft, black magic, malefic ties, maledictions, and the evil eye; diabolic infestations, oppressions, possessions; all that is evil and sinful, jealousy, perfidy, envy; physical, psychological, moral, spiritual, diabolical ailments.

Burn all these evils in Hell, that they may never again touch me or any other creature in the entire world.

I command and bind all the powers that molest me by the power of God All-Powerful, in the Name of Jesus Christ our Savior, through the intercession of the Immaculate Virgin Mary — to leave me forever and to be consigned into everlasting Hell, where they will be bound by St. Michael, St. Raphael, our Guardian Angels, and where they will be crushed under the heel of the Immaculate Virgin Mary. Amen.

Daily Devotion: Prayers for Healing of Person & Family

59. Psalm 91 Prayer

You who dwell in the shelter of the Most High, who abide in the shadow of the Almighty. say to the Lord, "My refuge and my fortress, My God, in whom I trust!" He will rescue you from the fowlers snare, from the destroying plague. He will shelter you with His pinions, and under His wings, you may take refuge; His faithfulness is a protecting shield. You shall not fear the terror of the night, nor of the arrow that flies by day, nor the pestilence that roams the darkness, nor the plague that ravages at noon. A thousand may fall at your side and ten thousand at your right hand; near you, it will not come. You need simply to watch. The punishment of the wicked you will see because you have the Lord for your refuge and have made the Most High your stronghold. No evil shall befall you; no affliction shall come near your tent. He commands His Angels with regard to you, to guard you wherever you go. With their hands, they shall support you, lest you strike your foot against a stone. You can tread upon the asp and the viper, trample the lion and the dragon "Because he clings to Me, and I will deliver him; because he has known My Name, I will set him on high. He will call upon Me, and I will answer him; I will be with him in distress; I will deliver him and give him honor. I will satisfy him with a long life and fill him with My Saving Power. Amen.

60. Commission of the Care of Soul and Body

Into thy hands, Mary, I commend my body and my soul. I ask thee to provide for them and to protect them. I ask thee to protect them from the evil one. I ask thee to enlighten my mind, strengthen my will, and refrain my appetites by grace. Our Lady and St. Michael, call down from Heaven the legions of Angels under your command to protect me; I ask of thee all the things I ask of my Guardian Angel. My Guardian Angel, under thy intellectual and volitional protection I place my body. I ask thee to illumine my mind and refrain my appetites. I ask thee to strengthen my cogitative power, my memory, and my imagination. Help me to remember the things I should and not remember the things I should not. Help me to associate the things I should and not to associate the things I should not. Give me good, clear images in my imagination. I ask thee to drive away all the demons that might affect me while I sleep (or throughout the course of the day). (Help me to sleep and, if thou should deem it prudent, direct my dreams. Help me to arise refreshed). Amen

61. Prayer of Blessing our Homes

O Father, come and visit our home (office, shop, etc.) and protect us from the lures of the enemy. May Your holy Angels come to guard our peace, and may Your blessing remain with us forever.

Entrust Your Angels to guard it and banish from it every evil power. Grant that all who live in it may please You with their good works and so receive from You, when their time comes, the reward of Your heavenly home. We ask this through Christ, our Lord. Amen.

Daily Devotion: Prayers for Healing of Person & Family

62. Home Blessing

Our help is in the Name of the Lord. Who made Heaven and earth. The Lord be with you. May He also be with you.

Let us pray. God the Father Almighty, we fervently implore You for the sake of this home and its occupants and possessions that You may bless and sanctify them, enriching them by Your kindness in every way possible. Pour out on them, Lord, heavenly dew in good measure, as well as an abundance of earthly needs. Mercifully listen to their prayers and grant that their desires be fulfilled. At our lowly coming, be pleased to bless and sanctify this home, as You once were pleased to bless the home of Abraham, Isaac, and Jacob. Within these walls, let Your Angels of light preside and stand watch over those who live here through Christ our Lord. Amen.

63. Mary, Bless This Home

O Mary, bless this home, where thy name is ever held in benediction. All glory to Mary, ever Immaculate, ever Virgin, blessed among women, the mother of our Lord, Jesus Christ, and Queen of Paradise. Cover this home with your mantle of protection. O Mother Mercy, pray for us. Amen.

64. I Consecrate My House

Most Blessed Virgin, whose heart is Sorrowful and Immaculate, we recognise thee as the Lady and Queen of this house.

Have kindness to preserve it from any evil: from fire, water, thunder, storms, earthquakes, from robbers, wicked people, from revolutionaries, war, raids, from persecution and taxes, from any other evil known to Thee.

Bless, protect, defend, and preserve as thy personal property those who live and will live here. Keep them away from adversity and misfortune, but above all, preserve them from offending God. Let not a single mortal sin be ever committed in this house. May all those who enter it work for the Glory of God, for the reign of Jesus and Mary.

Let this house be forever consecrated to you, O Jesus and Mary. Let it be blessed with all those who will inhabit it. Amen.

Daily Devotion: Spiritual Protection

65. Litany of Blessing Home

The Son of God, Lord of heaven and earth, came to deliver us from the power of the evil one. Let us call upon Him saying, **Lord, graciously hear us.**

Lord, Jesus Christ, by Your life with Mary and Joseph, You sanctify the life of the home and dwell in this home. Let Your blessings and protection be upon all who live here. Lord, hear us. **Lord, graciously hear us.**

Deliver this home from all snares of demons and keep all who swell here safe under the protection of Your wings, Lord; hear us, **Lord, graciously hear us.**

Deliver this home from all evil. You taught Your followers to build those homes on solid rock. Grant that the members of this family may hold fast to Your teachings and, freed of small discord, serve You with their whole hearts. Lord hear us, **Lord graciously hear us.**

Aided by the intercession of the Immaculate Virgin Mary and of Saint Michael the Archangel, may all who dwell in this home experience peace and joy. Lord hear us, **Lord graciously hear us.**

O Lord of God, hear our prayers we seek Your protection over all who dwell in this home. We ask You to drive out all unclean spirits and free this home from any evil presence or attachment. We make this prayer, Lord Jesus, in Your Holy Name. Amen.

66. Prayer for a Peaceful Home

Lord, Our God, hear our prayers. We seek your protection over all who dwell in this home. We ask you to drive out all unclean spirits and free this home from any evil presence or attachment. Hear us, Holy Lord, Father Almighty Everlasting God, in Your goodness, send Your Holy Angels from Heaven to watch over and protect all who live in this home, to be with them, and to give them comfort and encouragement through Christ Our Lord.

Pour Your blessings upon our home and make it a place of peace. May salvation enter our abode, as it entered the home of Zacchaeus when You graced it with Your presence. Entrust Your Holy Angels to guard it and to banish from it every evil power. Grant that all who live in it may please You with their good works and so receive from You in Your time comes the reward of Your heavenly home; we ask this through Christ Our Lord. Amen.

67. Prayer to Mary for Liberation

August Queen of Heaven, sovereign Queen of Angels, you who at the beginning received from God the power and the mission to crush the head of Satan, we humbly beseech you, send your heavenly legions so that on your orders and by your powers they will track down demons, fight them everywhere, curb their audacity, and plunge them into the abyss. O divine Mother, send us your Angels and Archangels to defend us, to watch over us. Holy Angels and Archangels defend us, protect us. Amen.

Daily Devotion: Spiritual Protection

68. Consecration of Exterior Goods to the Blessed Virgin Mary

I, (Name), a faithless sinner, renew and ratify today in thy hands the vows of my Baptism; I renounce forever satan, his pomps and works; and I give myself entirely to Jesus Christ, the Incarnate Wisdom, to carry my cross after Him all the days of my life, and to be more faithful to Him than I have ever been before.

In the presence of all the heavenly court, I choose thee, O Mary, this day for my Mother and Mistress. Knowing that I have received rights over all my exterior goods by the promulgation of the natural law, by the Divine Author, I deliver and consecrate to thee, as thy slave, all of my exterior goods past, present, and future, I relinquish into thy hands, my Heavenly Mother, all rights over my exterior goods, including my health, finances, relationships, possessions, property, my job, and my earthly success, (*mention here*) and I retain for myself no right of disposing of the goods that come to me but leave to thee the entire and full right of disposing of all that belongs to me, without exception, according to thy good pleasure, for the greater glory of God in time and in eternity.

As I now interiorly relinquish what belongs to me exteriorly into thy hands, I entrust to thee the protection of those exterior goods against the evil one so that, knowing that they now belong to thee, he cannot touch them.

Receive, O good and pious Virgin, this little offering of what little is, in honor of, and in union with, that subjection which the Eternal Wisdom deigned to have to thy maternity; in homage to the power which both of you have over this poor sinner, and in thanksgiving for the privileges with which the Holy Trinity has favored thee.

Trusting in the providential care of God the Father and thy

maternal care, I have full confidence that thou whilst take care of me as to the necessities of this life and will not leave me forsaken. God the Father, increase my trust in Thy Son's Mother; Our Lady of Fair Love, give me perfect confidence in the providence of Thy Son. Amen.

69. Prayer of Command

In His name and by the power of His Cross and Blood, I ask Jesus to bind any evil spirits, forces, and powers of the earth, air, fire, or water, of the netherworld and the satanic forces of nature. By the power of the Holy Spirit and by His authority, I ask Jesus Christ to break any curses, hexes, or spells and send them back to where they came from, if it be His Holy Will.

I beseech Thee, Lord Jesus, to protect us by pouring Thy Precious Blood on us (my family, etc.), which Thou hast shed for us, and I ask Thee to command that any departing spirits leave quietly, without disturbance and go straight to Thy Cross to dispose of as Thou sees fit.

I ask Thee to bind any demonic interaction, interplay, or communications. I place N. *(person, place, or thing)* under the protection of the Blood of Jesus Christ, which He shed for us. Amen.

70. Prayer for Breaking Ties

With the sword of St. Michael, the sword of Our Lady, and the sword of Our Lord's Cross, I sever and break any and all ties, bonds, and attachments not of Our Lord Jesus Christ. Amen.

71. Prayer for Deliverance

My Lord, You are All-Powerful, You are God, You are Father. We beg You through the intercession and help of the Archangels Saints, Michael, Raphael, and Gabriel, for the deliverance of our brothers and sisters who are enslaved by the evil one. All Saints of Heaven, come to our aid.

From anxiety, sadness, and obsessions, **we beg You, Free us, O Lord.**
From hatred, fornication, envy,...
From thoughts of jealousy, rage, and death...
From every thought of suicide and abortion...
From every form of sinful sexuality...
From every division in our family and every harmful friendship, we beg You, Free us, O Lord. From every sort of spell, malefic, witchcraft, and every form of the occult, we beg You, Free us, O Lord.

Lord, You Who said, "I leave you peace, My peace I give you," grant that, through the intercession of the Virgin Mary, we may be liberated from every evil spell and enjoy Your peace always. In the Name of Christ, our Lord. Amen.

72. Short Prayer Against Evil

In the Name of Jesus Christ, by the power of His Precious Blood, may any power or hold the devil has over me be utterly destroyed. May the Blessed Virgin Mary, St. Joseph- Terror of Demons, St. Michael with all the Angels and Saints be with me to protect me. Amen.

Daily Devotion: Spiritual Protection

73. Protection and Healing Prayer

Heavenly Father, I praise and thank You for all you have given me. Please cover me with the protective Precious Blood of Your Son, Jesus Christ, and increase Your Holy Spirit in me with His gifts of wisdom, knowledge, understanding, hunger for prayer, guidance, and discernment to help me know Your will and surrender to it more completely.

Father, please heal my negative emotions and any wounds in my heart and spirit. Send the Sword of Your Holy Spirit to sever and break all spells, curses, hexes, voodoo, and all negative genetic, intergenerational, and addictive material, past, present, or to come, known or unknown, against me, my relationships and family, finances, possessions, and ministry.

Father, I forgive and ask forgiveness for my sins and failings, and ask that my whole person, body and mind, heart and will, soul and spirit, memory and emotions, attitudes and values be cleansed, renewed, protected by the Most Precious Blood of Your Son, Jesus.

In the Name, Power, Blood, and Authority of Jesus Christ, I bind and break the power and effect in or around me of any and all evil spirits who are trying to harm me in any way, and I command these spirits and their companion spirits in the name of the Father, the Son, and the Holy Spirit **(+)** to leave me peacefully and quietly, and go immediately and directly to the Eucharistic Presence of Jesus Christ, in the closest Catholic Church Tabernacle, to be disposed of by Jesus and never again return to harm me. Jesus, please heal the effects of these spirits in and around me.

Dear Holy Spirit, please fill up any void in me to overflow with Your great love. All this, Father, I pray in the Name of Jesus Christ, by the guidance of Your Holy Spirit.

Immaculate Heart of Mary, Spouse of the Holy Spirit, please pray for and with me, in Jesus' Name, Amen.

74. Prayer for Deliverance
by Fr. Gabriel Amorth

O Jesus our Savior, my Lord and my God; my God and my all, with Your sacrifice on the Cross, You redeemed us and defeated the power of Satan. I beg You to deliver me from every evil presence and every evil influence.

I ask You in Your Name, I ask You for the sake of Your wounds, I ask You for the sake of Your Blood, I ask You for the sake of Your Cross, I ask You through the intercession of Mary, Immaculate and Sorrowful.

May the Blood and the Water that flow from Your side wash over me to purify me, deliver me, and heal me. Amen.

Daily Devotion: Spiritual Protection

75. Prayer for Release from Ancestral Curses
revealed to Barnabas Nwoye, attributed to Fr. Blount

Eternal Father, You are the Only Immortal God, God Who is Love, merciful, and kind. Look at Your only begotten Son, Jesus Christ, and have mercy on us. I offer You the pains of His scourging at the pillar, His Wounds and Blood for all Your people who are living under the weight of the curse due to the sins of their ancestors and their disobedience for breaking the covenant that You made with them. May You set us free through the scourging of Your Son, heal us through His Wounds, and save us through His Precious Blood.

Precious Blood of Jesus Christ, release me from all curses.
Holy Wounds of Jesus Christ, heal our wounds.
By Your scourging, heal us. Amen.

76. St. Joseph Protection Prayer

Saint Joseph, Terror of Demons, cast your solemn gaze upon the devil and all his minions and protect us with your mighty staff.

You fled through the night to avoid the devil's wicked designs; now, with the power of God, smite the demons as they flee from you. Grant special protection; we pray for children, fathers, families, the dying, our Rosary Family, and their loved ones.

By God's grace, no demon dare approach while you are near. So we beg of you, always be near us. Amen.

Priestly Thursdays

77. Night Salutation and Prayer to Jesus in the Tabernacle

O Divine Jesus, lonely tonight in so many Tabernacles, without visitor or worshiper, I offer You my heart. Oh, may its very beating be a prayer of love to You! You are always watching under the sacramental veils. In Your Love, You never sleep, and You are never weary of Your Vigils for sinners. O loving Jesus, O lonely Jesus, may my heart be a lamp, the light of which shall burn and beam for You alone! Watch, Sacramental Sentinel; watch for the weary world, for the erring soul, and for Your poor child! Amen.

Take a moment to think of every priest placed in your life.
Let's offer us this next part of our prayer for:

- *The priest who baptized us,*
- *The Bishop who confirmed us,*
- *Every priest who has heard our confession,*
- *Every priest who gave us Holy Communion, especially the priest who gave us our first Holy Communion.*
- *For sidelined priests, for our pastor and associate priests,*
- *For priests who feel lonely,*
- *Mentor priests,*
- *Priests who are emboldened,*
- *For priests who are losing their faith,*
- *For priests with addiction,*
- *For priests who are hurting or ill.*
- *We also pray for the priests we love or adopted to pray for (mention here).*

Priestly Thursdays

78. Chaplet of Reparation for Priests
To be prayed on the rosary

Begin: Incline (+) unto my aid, O Lord, make haste to help me. Glory be to the Father and to the Son and to the Holy Spirit As it was in the beginning, is now, and ever shall be, World without end. Amen.

Our Father Beads:
Eternal Father, I offer Thee the Precious Blood of Thy Beloved Son, Our Lord Jesus Christ, the Lamb without blemish or spot, in reparation for my sins and for the sins of all Thy priests.

Hail Mary Beads:
By Thy Precious Blood, O Jesus, purify and sanctify Thy priests.

Glory Be Beads:
O Father, from whom all fatherhood in heaven and on earth is named, Have mercy on all Thy priests and wash them in the Blood of the Lamb.

O Mary, Mother of the Clergy, pray for us.
St. John Vianney, Patron Saint of Priest, pray for us. Amen.

Priestly Thursdays

79. Prayer for Priests through the Intercessions of St. John Vianney, St. Padre Pio, St. John Bosco, St. Maximillian Kolbe, Venerable Fulton Sheen, & Servant of God Fr. John A. Hardon.

Most gracious Heavenly Father, we thank You for our faithful priests and bishops, whose spiritual fatherhood and example of fidelity, self-sacrifice, and devotion is so vital to the faith of Your people. May our spiritual fathers be guided by the examples of St. John Vianney, St. Padre Pio, St. John Bosco, St. Maximillian Kolbe, Venerable Fulton Sheen, and Servant of God Fr. John Anthony Hardon.

Give them valiant faith in the face of confusion and conflict, hope in times of trouble and sorrow, and steadfast love for You, their families, and all Your people throughout the world. May the light of Your Truth shine through their lives and their good works. Assist all spiritual fathers that through Your Grace, they may steadily grow in holiness and knowledge and understanding of Your Truth. May they generously impart this knowledge to those who rely on them. Through Christ our Lord. Amen.

St. John Vianney, St. Padre Pio, St. John Bosco, St. Maximillian Kolbe, Venerable Fulton Sheen, and Servant of God Fr. John Anthony Hardon- pray for us, especially your brother priests here on earth. Amen.

Prayers for Healing of Person & Family

Individual

80. Bless Me, Heavenly Father

Bless me, Heavenly Father, forgive my erring ways. Grant me strength to serve Thee, put purpose in my days. Give me understanding, enough to make me kind. So, I may judge all people with my heart, not my mind. Teach me to be patient in everything I do, content to trust Your wisdom, and to follow after You. Help me when I falter, hear me when I pray, And receive me in Thy kingdom to dwell with Thee someday. In Jesus' Name, I pray. Amen.

81. Holy Spirit Prayer
by St. Augustine

Breathe into me, Holy Spirit, that my thoughts may all be holy. Move in me, Holy Spirit, that my work, too, may be holy. Attract my heart, Holy Spirit, that I may love only what is holy. Strengthen me, Holy Spirit, that I may defend all that is holy. Protect me, Holy Spirit, that I may always be holy. Amen

82. Come Holy Spirit

Heavenly Father, in Jesus' Name, please let me be filled with the Holy Spirit to meet the challenges of the day. Wherever I go, let us spread love, joy, peace, goodness, and faith. Grant me the desire to become more like Jesus in all that I think, say, or do. Help us desire these things of Heaven more than the things of earth. Come Holy Spirit, come by means of the Flame of Love of the Immaculate Heart of Mary. Amen.

83. Powerful Prayer of Petition

Thou hast told us, O Lord Jesus, in the Holy Gospel, that "If you ask the Father anything in My Name, He will give it to you." Therefore, in Thy Name, relying upon Thy merits, and uniting myself to Thee, who art continually interceding for us in Heaven and in the Holy Eucharist, I ask the Father to grant all those graces necessary for me that I may ever do His Holy Will. Holy Father, seeing that Communion partakes of the efficacy of Holy Mass, which is the same as that of Calvary, I pray Thee, in the Name of Jesus Christ, to grant me all the graces that Thou wouldst have accorded me had I been at the foot of the Cross when Thy Divine Son died for us. His blood was shed for us; therefore, may its saving power reach all souls, and may they be gathered to Thee. Give to me, O God, and to all men Thy grace in this world and Thy glory in the next. Amen.

84. Serenity Prayer

God, grant me the serenity to accept the things I cannot change, the courage to change the things I can, and the wisdom to know the difference.

Living one day at a time, enjoying one moment at a time; accepting hardship as a pathway to peace; taking, as Jesus did, this sinful world as it is, not as I would have it; trusting that You will make all things right if I surrender to Your will; so that I may be reasonably happy in this life and supremely happy with You forever in the next. Amen.

85. Learning Christ

Teach me, my Lord, to be sweet and gentle in all the events of life: in disappointments, in the thoughtlessness of others, in the insincerity of those I trusted, in the unfaithfulness of those on whom I relied. Let me put myself aside to think of the happiness of others, to hide my little pains and heartaches so I may be the only one to suffer them. Teach me to profit by the suffering that comes across my path. Let me so use it that it may mellow me, not harden nor embitter me; that it may make me patient, not irritable, that it may make me broad in my forgiveness, not narrow, haughty, and overbearing.

May no one be less good for having come within my influence. No one is less pure, less noble for having been a fellow traveler in our journey toward eternal life. As I go my rounds from one distraction to another, let me whisper, from time to time, a word of love to You. May our life be lived in the supernatural, full of power for good, and strong in its purpose of sanctity. Amen

86. Prayer in Union With Jesus

Lord Jesus, grant me the grace to empty myself and be filled with Your love, peace, patience, compassion, mercy, forgiveness, and understanding. Let every beat of my heart and every breath that I breathe be for You. Let every word that I speak be reflective of You. Let every glance I give be a mirror of You. Let every hand I touch feel Your gentle care. Let every step I take be on Your path toward Your light. Let every word of praise I may receive be directed to You in humble thanksgiving. Let every angry word said to me or against me be returned with words of love and mercy, not anger and revenge. Let every desire I have be for You. Let my will conform to Yours. Touch every cell of my body, Lord, and make me the person, the servant You want me to be. Amen.

87. Prayer for Union With Jesus

Come to me, Lord, and possess my soul. Come into my heart and permeate my soul. Help me to sit in silence with You and let You work in my heart.

I am Yours to possess. I am Yours to use. I want to be selfless and only exist in You. Help me to spoon out all that is me and be an empty vessel ready to be filled by You. Help me to die to myself and live only for You. Use me as You will. Let me never draw my attention back to myself. I only want to operate as You do, dwelling within me.

I am Yours, Lord. I want to have my life in You. I want to do the will of the Father. Give me the strength to put aside the world and let You operate my very being. Help me to act as You desire. Strengthen me against the distractions of the devil to take me from Your work.

When I worry, I have taken my focus off of You and placed it on myself. Help me not to give into the promptings of others to change what is in my heart. You are making it very clear to me. I worship You. I adore You, and I love You. Come and dwell in me now. Amen.

88. A Healing Prayer

Heavenly Father, I call on You right now in a special way. It is through Your power that I was created. Every breath I take, every morning I wake, and every moment of every hour, I live under Your loving power. Father, we ask You now to touch me with that same power: You created me from nothing, You can certainly recreate me. Fill me with the healing power of Your Spirit. Cast out anything that should not be in me. Mend what is broken. Root out any unproductive cells. Open any blocked arteries or veins and rebuild any damaged areas. Remove all inflammation and cleanse any infection. Let the warmth of Your healing love pass through my body to make new any unhealthy areas so that my body will function the way You created it to function. And Father, restore me to full health in mind, body, and spirit so that I may serve You the rest of my life with great love and zeal. I ask this through Christ, Our Lord. Amen

89. Short Healing Prayer

Heavenly Father, in Jesus' Holy Name and by the power of the Holy Spirit, drive away all spirits of infirmity and disease from me. Give strength to my body and joy to my soul so that in my renewed health, I may bless and serve You, now and forever. O Mary conceived without sin, pray for us who have recourse to thee. Amen

90. Prayer of St. Gertrude for Sleeplessness

I beseech Thee, O Most Merciful God, by the most tranquil sweetness with which Thou hast reposed from all eternity in the bosom of the Father, by Thy peaceful abode of nine months in the womb of a virgin, and by all the holy delights which Thou hast ever enjoyed in souls filled with Thy love, to grant me some rest, not for my own satisfaction, but for Thy eternal glory, so that the strength of my wearied body may be restored, and that I may be able to fulfill my duties. Amen.

91. Healing Prayer at Bedtime

Lord Jesus, through the power of the Holy Spirit, go back into my memory as I sleep.

- Every hurt that has ever been done to me heal that hurt.
- Every hurt that I have ever caused another person to heal that hurt.
- All the relationships that have been damaged in my whole life that I am unaware of heal those relationships.

But Lord, if there is anything I need to do, if I need to go to a person because he or she is still suffering from my hand, bring to my awareness that person, I choose to forgive, and I ask to be forgiven. Remove whatever bitterness may be in my heart, Lord, and fill the empty spaces with Your love. Amen

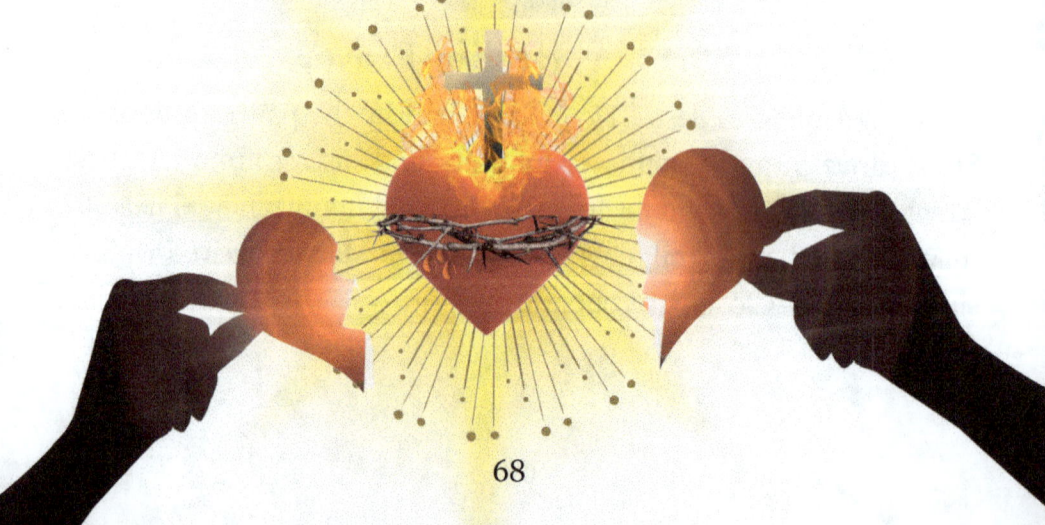

Healing: Specific

92. Prayer of St Gertrude the Great, Before Work

O Lord Jesus Christ, in union with Your most perfect actions, I commend to You this my work, to be directed according to Your adorable will, for the salvation of all mankind. Amen.

93. Holy Spirit Tension Prayer

Come, Holy Spirit, replace the tension within us with a holy relaxation. Replace the turbulence within us with a sacred calm. Replace the anxiety within us with a quiet confidence. Replace the fear within us with a strong faith. Replace the bitterness within us with the sweetness of grace. Replace the darkness within us with a gentle light. Replace the coldness within us with a loving warmth. Replace the night within us with Your light. Replace the winter within us with Your spring. Straighten our crookedness. Fill our emptiness, dull the edge of our pride. Sharpen the edge of our humility. Light the fires of our love. Quench the flames of our lust. Let us see ourselves as You see us, that we may see You as You have promised, And be fortunate according to Your word, "Blessed are the pure of heart, for they shall see God." Amen.

94. Prayer During Difficult Times

God of love and mercy, assist me in this time of trouble and anxiety. Ease my burdens. Strengthen my faith. Increase my trust and confidence in Your compassionate care. Give me the courage I need, dear Lord, to face the difficulties before me, knowing that with Your help, miracles happen and lives are restored. I pray for a share in Your healing graces and ask that You surround me with Your comforting goodness, for health in mind and body, and for a heart filled with hope and peace. Amen.

Daily Devotion: Prayers for Healing of Person & Family

95. Payer to Mary for Protection Against Danger

Mother of Jesus, be our protector and defender against all that is harmful or evil. Bring our needs before Almighty God so that we may be surrounded by God's Holy Angels, and give us the grace to conquer every danger and overcome all that would threaten our health and well-being.

Be for us light in times of darkness, strength when we are weak, wisdom in our confusion, healing in times of illness, and courage to work through life's problems and difficulties. Give us joy when we are sad, bread to feed our hunger, and eternal life to defeat the power of death.
Virgin Mary, guide our life journey so that we may always walk safely together with you and your Divine Son, Jesus Christ, in God's loving friendship. Amen.

96. Prayer for Daily Challenges

Heavenly Father, in Jesus' Name, please let me be filled with the Holy Spirit to meet the challenges of today. Wherever I go, let me spread love, joy, peace, goodness, and faith. Grant me the desire to become more like Jesus in all that I think, say, and do. Help me to desire these things of Heaven more than the things of earth... Come Holy Spirit! Come by means of the power of the Flame of Love of the Immaculate Heart of Mary! Amen.

97. Prayer for Enemies

God our Father, Your Son, commanded us, "Love your enemies and pray for those who persecute you." By dying for all humanity and asking You to forgive those who crucified Him, Jesus saved us and made us sons and daughters of God.

Following His example, we pray for our enemies, known and unknown. We ask that the loving will of God be done in their lives. May the Holy Spirit come into their lives and transform their hearts and ours, leading to peace and reconciliation amongst all Your children. In Jesus' name, we pray. Amen.

98. Prayer to Redeem Lost Time
by St. Teresa of Avila

O my God! Source of all mercy! I acknowledge Your sovereign power. While recalling the wasted years that are past, I believe that You, Lord, can, in an instant, turn this loss into gain. Miserable as I am, yet I firmly believe that You can do all things. Please restore to me the time lost, giving me Your grace, both now and in the future, that I may appear before You in "wedding garments." Amen.

99. Prayer for Health

Heavenly Father, in Jesus' Holy Name and by the power of the Holy Spirit, drive away all spirits of infirmity and disease from me. Give strength to my body and joy to my soul so that in my renewed health, I may bless and serve You, now and forever.

O Mary, conceived without sin, pray for us who have recourse to thee. Amen.

100. Prayer for Healing

Lord, look upon me with eyes of mercy. May Your Healing Spirit rest upon me. It is through Your power that I was created. Since You created me from nothing, You can certainly recreate me. Fill me with the healing power of Your spirit. May Your life-giving powers flow into every cell of my body and into the depths of my soul. Mend what is broken. Cast out anything that should not be within me. Rebuild my brokenness.

Restore my strength for service in Your Kingdom. Touch my soul with Your compassion for others. Touch my heart with Your courage and infinite love for all. Touch my mind with Your wisdom, that my mouth may always proclaim Your praise. Teach me to reach out to You in my need, and help me to lead others to You by my example. Most loving Heart of Jesus, bring me health in body and spirit that I may serve You with all my strength. Amen.

Daily Devotion: Prayers for Healing of Person & Family

101. Prayer of Charity

Gracious God, I offer You my heartfelt gratitude for Your countless graces and blessings to me and my loved ones each day. In response to Your goodness, dear Lord, help me be aware of the needs of my brothers and sisters and assist those who are poor and less fortunate with generous expressions of charity, kindness, and caring.

On that day, Lord, when I finally stand before You to give an account of my life, I pray I will hear You say, "Come, O good and faithful servant, to share your Father's joy, for when I was hungry, thirsty, naked, homeless ill and imprisoned," you offered your gifts in charity and lovingly did it for Me. Amen.

102. Prayer for Courage in Suffering

Jesus, even though You never committed any fault, You lived a life of suffering. You took upon Yourself all our sins. You started Your life in a cold stable. You began Your public life with a severe fast. You shed Your Blood for love of me and a hideous death on the cross.

Lord, I seek a willingness to deny myself and take up my and others' crosses daily. Grant me a spirit of mortification so I, too, can live my life like Yours. Help me to be willing to shed tears for those whom You entrusted to my care. Amen.

103. Gratitude in Suffering

O my God, I thank You for this cross You have allowed me to carry. Please give me the strength and faith to persevere so that I may bring glory to Your name while withstanding the burden of its weight. Thank You for offering me a share in Your suffering. I know that You have always been, are now, and ever will be at my side every step of the way. Thank You also for every "Simon" that You have sent to help me bear this cross. I have prayed so often that this thorn in my flesh would be removed, but I trust that your grace is sufficient. Change my heart's troubled cry of "How long, O Lord?" into words of trust: "However long, O Lord."

May I seek only to do Your will and to unite my sufferings with Your passion. Help me not to get lost in my self-concerns, but may I find in these trials a way to greater virtue, a call to prayer, and a path to trust in You alone. Permit me not to waste my pain but to make of these struggles a sacrificial offering for others. Lord, when I am weary, and I fall, exhausted under the weight of this cross, please give me the courage to press on as You did. Lord Jesus, I embrace with love my cross as a share in Your own. By Your grace, may I carry it all the way to the vision of Your Glory. I abandon myself totally to Your will. Christ Jesus, I trust in you. Amen.

Family

104. Prayer for Marriages

Dear Lord, we thank You and praise You for the gift of marriage. We humbly ask You to pour out Your grace upon all marriages. The married state can be very difficult and demanding at times. You know all the deepest struggles and temptations couples face. You call them to rely on You to overcome the problems. In marriage, You call spouses to love a selfless and sacrificial love. Help them to accomplish this, even in the most difficult of circumstances. Strengthen and bless all marriages., and those preparing for the Holy Sacrament of Marriage. Help couples to grow in true love for You, for each other, all the days of their life. Amen.

105. Prayer for Healing My Family

Loving Lord, You are the God of all time and space, so I pray for my family through all generations: those who have lived, those who are living, and those who are yet to be born. And I ask that You heal us, O Lord, in all the ways You know we are most in need of healing. Most Sacred Heart of Jesus, I place my family through all generations in Your loving care. Amen.

Daily Devotion: Prayers for Healing of Person & Family

106. Prayer for Broken Families

God our healer, we lift up to You in prayer all families who are divided or broken by human failure. We ask that You draw forth the pains caused by divorce, infidelity, abandonment, and selfishness as one draws out a poison and begin the healing that is needed in the hearts of Your people. May the households of humanity be places of reconciliation, forgiveness, and peace.

Lord, restore broken relationships, inspire forgiveness in the wronged, and heal the restlessness and inner pains of those who have divided their families. Inspire those affected by familial brokenness to pray at all times for Your will to be done, both now and in the future. We ask this in the Name of Jesus Christ, by Whose own wounds we are healed. Amen.

107. Prayer to St. Joseph, Protector of Families

St. Joseph, protect our home. Pour forth heaven's blessings upon each member of our family. Remain in our midst. Help us to live in love, harmony, peace, joy, prayer, and faith. May the wholesome fear of God strengthen us, that virtue may adorn what we do, and our way may lead to heaven. To you this day, I give the key to our dwelling place. Lock out all things that could do us harm. Lock my home and loved ones in the Hearts of Jesus and Mary. This I beg of you, that our days may be like your days in the holy home of Nazareth. Amen.

Daily Devotion: Prayers for Healing of Person & Family

108. Prayer for Family Peace & Unity at Gatherings

Heavenly Father, in Jesus' Name and by the Power of the Holy Spirit aid my family members to have peace and unity with each other. Bless our family gatherings. Help each of my family members accept and practice the core values of our Faith for the betterment of us all. O Blessed Mother and St. Joseph please let everybody feel loved and respected in the family. Let us be dedicated to the good of one another at all times. Dear Lord, let us not hold on to anger or unforgiveness in our hearts, for it will lead to resentment, bitterness, and even hatred. Teach us how to solve our conflicts openly, honestly, and promptly. Please help us to be humble enough to admit our failures and to seek forgiveness, love and peace when we have done wrong to others. Jesus, Mary, & Joseph, please help each of us to find peace so as to maintain the unity of the family. Amen.

Place a picture of your family here to hold in constant prayer.

109. Prayer for Protection Against Curses, Harm, and Accidents
(adapted)

Lord Jesus, I ask Thee to protect my family from sickness, from all harm, and from accidents. If any of us has been subjected to any curses, hexes, or spells, I beg Thee to declare these curses, hexes, or spells null and void. If any evil spirits have been sent against us, I ask that these evil spirits be sent to the foot of Your Cross to be dealt with as You will. Then, Lord, I ask Thee to send Thy Holy Angels to guard and protect all of us. Amen.

110. Healing of the Family Tree

Dear Lord Jesus, I ask you to stand between me and my ancestors to the fourth generation. Cut off all bondages and place all my ancestors in Your five Most Precious Wounds. I ask You to cleanse, purify, and free me of my ancestors' inheritance from any curse, voodoo, disorder, bondage, masonic ties, or generational spirits as they pass through Your Holy Wounds. May I receive my inheritance free from any bondages, cover and seal me in Your Precious Blood, that I may be completely free forever. O Blessed Virgin Mary, crush the head of the devil. Amen.

111. Release from Ancestral curses

Lord, we ask that You would break the curse of addiction, the curse of violence, and any other curse that has been passed down through our families. Cut, destroy, and sever any generational curses or inclinations we have developed in our blood lineage.

Precious Blood of Jesus Christ—release us from generational curses.
Holy Wounds of Jesus Christ—heal our wounds.
By Your scourging—seal us. Amen.

Daily Devotion: Prayers for Healing of Person & Family

112. Invocation Flame of Love

Heart of Jesus, burning with love for us, enflame our hearts with love of You. Amen.

113. A Spiritual Communion to make for EACH Member of your Family

SINGLE:

My Jesus, help ***(name of family member)*** to believe deeply, that Thou art truly present in the Most Blessed Sacrament. Grant *(name)* to love Thee above all things and to long for Thee in *his/her* soul. If *he/she* cannot now receive thee sacramentally, please come at least spiritually into *his/her* heart. Inspire *him/her* to embrace Thee, and to unite *himself/herself* entirely to Thee. Never permit *him/her* to be separated from Thee. Amen.

MULTIPLE:

My Jesus, help ***(names of family members)*** to believe deeply, that Thou art truly present in the Most Blessed Sacrament. Grant each of them individually to love Thee above all things and to long for Thee in each of their souls. If they cannot now receive Thee sacramentally, please come at least spiritually into each of their hearts. Inspire ***(names of family members)*** to embrace Thee, and to unite themselves entirely to Thee. Never permit them to be separated from Thee. Amen.

**Jesus asked for this in the Flame of Love Diary (simplified version) p. 18: "On Tuesday, pray for the family and make Spiritual Communions for each member. My Mother will take each under her protection. Offer night prayer for them. Invoke St. Joseph. He will help you."

114. A Parent's Prayer
by Msgr Stephen Rossettin (adapted)

Heavenly Father, I invoke the full authority You have given me as a spouse and a parent, and I renounce any curses, spells, seals, hexes, vexes, consecrations, voodoo, or any occult action or any evil affecting me or my spouse or my children who are minors.

In Jesus' name, I cast out all evil spirits that are harming us. In Jesus' name, I reject them, I rebuke them, I renounce them, and I cast them out!

For my adult children, I beg you, Heavenly Father, to hear a parent's plea and free them from any of these occult actions or any evil. Cast out all evil spirits! Father, I beseech You to send the spirit of peace and unity to my family. Heal the divisions in our family. May those family members who are estranged from each other be reconciled in forgiveness and love. May we live together in Your peace.

I pray for special healing grace for each one of us. Heal the wounds that plague us. Heal any depression. Heal all anxiety, fears, compulsions, addictions, anger, resentment, and any and all mental and physical illnesses. Restore us to full health.

I especially ask for the following and specific graces for my family, if it be Your Holy Will (*mention here*). Most of all, may You infuse the gift of faith into our hearts, always trusting in You. Bring back any of us who have wandered from the faith. May we be protected from all harm and evil by the shield of faith and the sword of truth. I make this parent's prayer in the Holy Name of Jesus Christ, begging the powerful intercession of the Holy Family with the Virgin Mary and St. Joseph and all the Saints. Amen.

115. Miscarriage Prayer
by Mother Angelica

My Lord, the baby is dead! Why, my Lord, dare I ask why? It will not hear the whisper of the wind or see the beauty of its parents' faces. It will not see the beauty of Your creation or the flame of a sunrise. Why, my Lord?

"Why, My child, do you ask 'why'? Well, I will tell you why.

You see, the child lives. Instead of the wind, he hears the sound of Angels singing before My throne. Instead of the beauty that passes, he sees everlasting Beauty; he sees My face. He was created and lived a short time, so the image of his parents imprinted on his face may stand before Me as their personal intercessor. He knows secrets of heaven unknown to men on earth. He laughs with a special joy that only the innocent possess. My ways are not the ways of man. I create for My Kingdom, and each creature fills a place in that Kingdom that could not be filled by another. He was created for My joy and his parents' merits. He has never seen pain or sin. He has never felt hunger or pain. I breathed a soul into a seed, made it grow, and called it forth."

I am humbled before You, my Lord, for questioning Your wisdom, goodness, and love. I speak as a fool; forgive me. I acknowledge Your sovereign rights over life and death. I thank You for the life that began for so short a time to enjoy so long an Eternity. Amen.

116. Prayer for the Gift of Children/Grandchildren Through the Intercession of St. Gianna Beretta Molla

St. Gianna, you are an incredible example of motherhood, selflessness, and devotion to God. Please fill us with your piety, your charity, and your goodness. St. Gianna, you were filled with love for your children. You understand the longing in our hearts for children. You understand our desire for a family filled with love and the giggles of babies and little ones. Please, St. Gianna, in your compassion, as a mother, wife, and a Saint of the Church, intercede on our behalf to our Lord, Christ Jesus. Help *(name here)* conceive or adopt a child. Whatever God's Holy Will is for our/their family.

Blessed St. Gianna, hear our prayers and ask that God, in His Mercy, grant our request for a healthy baby, a healthy child, that will be raised to be a loving child of God. In Jesus' Name. Amen.

117. Prayer for the Recovery of a Sick Person

Most merciful Jesus, who are the consolation and salvation of all who put their trust in You, we humbly beseech You, by Your most bitter Passion, to grant the recovery of health to Your servant *(name here)*, provided this be for their soul's welfare, that with us they may praise and magnify Your Holy Name. Amen.

118. Prayer for Those Suffering from Addiction

God of life, You made each of us in Your perfect image to live in Your love and to give You glory, honor, and praise. God of Mercy, give Your strength to anyone suffering from addiction, bounded by the chains of their addiction. Enfold them in Your love and restore them to the freedom as Your child. Open their hearts to Your healing power. Come, Lord Jesus, calm their soul just as You whispered "Peace" to the stormy sea.

Mary, our Mother, I beg You to intercede for me that they may find strength to overcome their illness. Bless all those who struggle with addiction. Touch them, heal them, reassure them of the Father's constant love. Remain at their side to drive away all evil temptations, fears, and doubts. May the quiet assurance of your loving presence illuminate the darkness in their heart and bring lasting peace. Amen.

119. Prayer to Mother Mary for those Suffering with Cancer

Mary, health of the sick, you brought forth into our world Jesus Christ, our Divine Healer. In your caring goodness, intercede for *(name here)*, who truly needs miraculous assistance.

If it is God's will, I ask this day that the gift of healing from all forms of cancer be granted to *(name)*. Comfort them during times of anguish, pain, confusion, and despair. Ask our gracious Savior to grant them physical health, inner peace, and patience in suffering. May God's healing graces grant *(name)* a life of happiness, health, and fulfillment here on earth and one day the joy of eternal glory in His loving embrace. Amen.

Daily Devotion: Prayers for Healing of Person & Family

120. The Purple Scapular Prayer

I hail Thee, Jesus crucified, for granting me life. I hail Thee with all the joy of the Angels and Saints during Your descent from the Cross. I hail Thee with the sadness of your mother while You rested on her Immaculate Heart and lap.

O Crux Ave, spes unica, et Verbum caro factum est.
O Jesus, conqueror of death, save us! Amen (5xs)

121. Healing Prayer Precious Blood of Jesus

Heavenly Father, in the Name of Jesus Thy Son, I pray: May the Precious Blood of Jesus wash over and through me. Let it heal every wound and scar so that the devil may find no purchase in me. Cause it to saturate and fill up my whole being: my heart, soul, mind, and body; my memory and my imagination; my past and my present; every fiber of my being, every molecule, every atom. Let there remain no part of me untouched by His Precious Blood. Make it flow over and around the altar of my heart on every side. Fill and heal, especially the wounds and scars of/caused by *(mention here)*. These things I ask of You, Heavenly Father, in the Name of Jesus through Mary's intercession. Amen.

122. Prayer for Peace

O Jesus, Prince of Peace, we come to You. O Mary, Queen of Peace, we come to you to intercede. O St. Joseph, Guardian of Peace in our homes, we come to you to intercede.

Eternal Holy God, we come to You burdened with worries, fears, doubts, anxieties, and troubles. Calm and quiet me with peace of heart and mind. Empty me of all my anxieties that disturb me, all the concerns that weary my spirit and weigh heavily on my mind and heart. Loosen my grip on the disappointments, grievances, and illusions of control that I hold on to so tightly. Release me from the pain of my past hurts, of present anger, and the tension of future fears. Sometimes, it is too much for me, Lord, too many demands, too many problems with sadness and suffering and stress. Sometimes, it overwhelms me, weighs me down, or I just want to give up.

I pray that you renew me, Lord. Renew me spiritually, that I may feel Your peace and turn to You. Renew me emotionally so I may be as loving as You when those stresses arise. Renew me with strength, hope, confidence, wisdom, and understanding. Grant me the graces to meet the constant struggles of daily life with a deeper faith and a deeper trust in You. Jesus, I trust in You to take care of everything. Amen.

123. Prayer for Those in Their Last Agony

O most merciful Jesus, Lover of souls, I pray Thee, by the agony of Thy Most Sacred Heart, and by the sorrows of Thy Immaculate Mother, cleanse in Thine Own Blood the sinners of the whole world who are now in their agony and to die this day.

O Heart of Jesus, once in agony, have pity on the dying. Amen.

124. Prayer for the Recently Departed

O Loving Father, Source of all Life, please accompany Your servant who recently passed from this earth to the kingdom of heavenly peace to rest in Eternal Life that You prepared. Forgive any sins that they have committed and welcome these departed souls into the joyful embrace of Your never-ending love. Amen.

Daily Devotion: Prayers for Healing of Person & Family
125. Prayer to One's Guardian Angel for a Happy Death
by St. Charles Borromeo

My Good Angel: I know not when or how I shall die. It is possible I may be carried off suddenly and that before my last sigh, I may be deprived of all intelligence. Yet, there are many things I would wish to say to God on the threshold of eternity. In the full freedom of my will today, I come to charge you to speak for me at that fearful moment. You will say to Him, then, O my Good Angel: That I wish to die in the Roman Catholic Apostolic Church in which all the Saints since Jesus Christ have died, and out of which there is no salvation.

That I ask the grace of sharing in the infinite merits of my Redeemer and that I desire to die in pressing to my lips the Cross that was bathed in His Blood!

That I detest my sins because they displease Him, and that I pardon through love of Him all my enemies as I wish myself to be pardoned.

That I die willingly because He orders it, and that I throw myself with confidence into His adorable Heart, awaiting all His Mercy.

That in my inexpressible desire to go to Heaven, I am disposed to suffer everything it may please His Sovereign Justice to inflict on me.

That I love Him before all things, above all things, and for His own sake; that I wish and hope to love Him with the Elect, His Angels, and the Blessed Mother during all eternity.

Do not refuse, O my Angel, to be my interpreter with God and to protest to Him that these are my sentiments and my will. Amen.

Monthly Devotions & Novenas

15 Promises of the Rosary

Promises 6-10

6. Those who recite my Rosary devoutly, applying themselves to the consideration of its sacred mysteries, shall never be conquered by misfortune. In His justice, God will not chastise them, nor shall they perish by an unprovided death, i.e., be unprepared for heaven. Sinners shall convert. The just shall persevere in grace and become worthy of eternal life.
7. Those who have a true devotion to the Rosary shall not die without the sacraments of the Church.
8. Those who faithfully recite the Rosary shall have, during their life and at their death, the light of God and the plenitude of His graces. At the moment of death, they shall participate in the merits of the Saints in paradise.
9. I shall deliver from purgatory those who have been devoted to the Rosary.
10. The faithful children of the Rosary shall merit a high degree of glory in heaven.

First Wednesdays

126. Consecration to St. Joseph

O dearest St. Joseph, I consecrate myself to your honor and give myself to you that you may always be my father, my protector, and my guide in the way of salvation. Obtain for me a greater purity of heart and fervent love for the interior life. After thine example, may I do all my actions for the greater glory of God, in union with the Divine Heart of Jesus and the Immaculate Heart of Mary! And do thou, O Blessed St. Joseph, pray for me that I may share in the peace and joy of thy holy death. Amen.

127. Consecration to the Heart of St. Joseph

My glorious St. Joseph, by the graces of thy Most Chaste Heart, save the Holy Catholic Church against the attacks of Satan and defend, with the intercession and power, devotion to the Hearts of Jesus and Mary, for God hath granted you great power and glory! I want to be thy servant for love of Jesus and Mary, for life.

To Your Most Chaste Heart, we consecrate ourselves today, O Glorious Saint Joseph. We consecrate our families and all that we have. The way you protected Jesus and Mary, protect also, my beloved protector, my soul, and my life against the dangers that surround me and attack me. O Glorious Saint Joseph, teach me to love deeply the Most Holy Hearts of Jesus and Mary so that as they, I will also come to love deeply your Most Chaste Heart, honoring it and making it known as you deserve to be honored and loved for all eternity. Amen!

First Wednesdays: Holy Cloak Novena

128. Holy Cloak of St. Joseph Novena

*Parts of the Novena may be used throughout the year in prayer.

Offering 1: O Glorious Patriarch St. Joseph, I humbly prostrate myself before you. I beg the Lord Jesus, your Immaculate Spouse, the Blessed Virgin Mary, and all the Angels and Saints in the Heavenly Court to join me in this devotion. I offer you this precious cloak while pledging my sincerest faith and devotion. I promise to do all in my power to honor you throughout my lifetime to prove my love for you.

Help me, St. Joseph. Assist me now and throughout my lifetime, but especially at the moment of my death, as you were assisted by Jesus and Mary, that I may join you one day in Heaven and there honor you for all eternity. Amen.

Offering 2: O Glorious Patriarch St. Joseph, I prostrate before you and your Divine Son Jesus; we offer you with heartfelt devotion this precious treasury of prayers, being ever mindful of the numerous virtues which adorned your sacred person. In you, O Glorious Patriarch, has fulfilled the dream of your precursor, the first Joseph, who indeed seemed to have been sent by God to prepare the way for your presence on this earth. In fact, not only were you surrounded by the shining splendor of the rays of the Divine Sun, Jesus, but you were splendidly reflected in the brilliant light of the mystic moon, the Blessed Virgin Mary. O Glorious Patriarch, if the example of the ancient Jacob, who personally went to congratulate his favorite son, who was exalted on the throne of Egypt, served to bring all his progeny there, should not the example of Jesus and Mary, who honored you with their greatest respect and trust, serve to bring us, your devoted servants, to present you with this precious cloak in your honor.

Grant, O great St. Joseph, that the Almighty God may turn a benevolent glance toward us. As the ancient Joseph did not reject his guilty and cruel brothers but rather accepted them with love and protected and saved them from hunger and death, we beseech you, O Glorious Patriarch, through your intercession, grant that the Lord may never abandon us in this exiled valley of sorrows. Grant that He may always number us among your devoted servants who live serenely under the patronage of your Holy Cloak. Grant that we may live always within the protection of this patronage every day of our lives particularly at that moment when we draw our dying breath.

Prayer 1: Hail, O Glorious St. Joseph, you who are entrusted with the priceless treasures of Heaven and earth and foster-father of Him who nourishes all the creatures of the universe. You are, after Mary, the Saint most worthy of our love and devotion. You alone, above all the Saints, were chosen for that supreme honor of rearing, guiding, nourishing, and even embracing the Messiah, whom so many kings and prophets would have so desired to behold.

St. Joseph, save our souls and obtain for us from the Divine Mercy of God that petition for which we humbly pray. And for the Holy Souls in Purgatory, grant a great comfort from their pain. Amen.

Prayer 2: O powerful St. Joseph, you were proclaimed the Patron of the Universal Church; therefore, we invoke you, above all the other Saints, as the greatest protector of the afflicted, and we offer countless blessings to your most generous heart, always ready to help in any need.

To you, O Glorious St. Joseph, come the widows, the orphans, the abandoned, the afflicted, the oppressed. There is no sorrow, heartache, or anguish which you have not consoled. Deign, we beseech you to use on our behalf those gifts which God has given you until we, too, shall be granted the answer to our petition. And you, Holy Souls in Purgatory, pray to St. Joseph for us. Amen.

Prayer 3: Countless are those who have prayed to you before us and have received comfort and peace, graces and favors. Our hearts, so sad and sorrowful, cannot find rest in the midst of this trial which besets us. O Glorious St. Joseph, you know all our needs even before we set them forth in prayer. You know how important this petition is for us. We prostrate ourselves before you as we sigh under the heavy weight of the problem which confronts us.

There is no human heart in which we can confide our sorrow, and even if we should find a compassionate creature who would be willing to assist us, still he would be unable to help us. Only you can help us in our sorrow, St. Joseph, and we beg you to hear our plea.

Has not St. Teresa left it written in her Dialogues that the world may always know, "Whatever you ask of St. Joseph, you shall receive"?

O St. Joseph, comforter of the afflicted, have pity on our sorrow and pity on those Poor Souls who place so much hope in you. Amen.

First Wednesdays: Holy Cloak Novena

Prayer 4: O Sublime Patriarch St. Joseph, because of your perfect obedience to God, you may intercede for us.

For your holy life full of grace and merit, hear our prayer.
For your most sweet name, help us. For your most holy tears, comfort us. For your seven sorrows, intercede for us. For your seven joys, console us. From all harm of body and soul, deliver us. From all danger and disaster, save us.

Assist us with your powerful intercession and seek for us, through your power and mercy, all that is necessary for our salvation and particularly the favor of which we now stand in such great need. Amen.

Prayer 5: O Glorious St. Joseph, countless are the graces and favors which you have obtained for afflicted souls. Those who suffer illness of every nature, those who are oppressed, persecuted, betrayed, bereft of all human comfort, even those in need of their life bread—all who implore your powerful intercession are comforted in their affliction.

Do not permit, O dearest St. Joseph, that we alone be the only ones of all who have appealed to you to be denied this petition, which we so earnestly beg of you. Show your kindness and generosity even to us, that we may cry out in thanksgiving, "Eternal glory to our Holy Patriarch St. Joseph, our great protector on earth and the defender of the Holy Souls in Purgatory." Amen.

Prayer 6: Eternal Father, Who art in Heaven, through the merits of Jesus and Mary, we beg You to grant our petition. In the name of Jesus and Mary, we prostrate ourselves before Your Divine Presence, and we beseech You to accept our hopeful plea to persevere in our prayers that we may be numbered among the throngs of those who live under the patronage of St. Joseph.

Extend Your blessing on this precious treasury of prayers which we today offer to him as a pledge of our devotion. Amen.

128.1 Memorare of St. Joseph

Remember, O most chaste spouse of the Blessed Virgin Mary, our good protector, St. Joseph, that never was it known that anyone who came to your protection and sought your intercession was left unaided. Confidently, we prostrate ourselves before you and fervently beg for your powerful intervention. O foster-father of our dear Redeemer, despise not our petition, but in your mercy hear and answer us. Amen.

128.2 Invocation to St. Joseph

Glorious St. Joseph, Spouse of the Blessed Virgin Mary and virginal father of Jesus, look upon us and watch over us; lead us on the path of sanctifying grace; take heed of the urgent needs which we now beg you to envelop within the folds of your fatherly cloak. Dismiss those obstacles and difficulties standing in the way of our prayers and grant that the happy answer to our petition may serve for the greater glory of God and our eternal salvation. Amen.

First Wednesdays: Holy Cloak Novena

128.3 Closing Prayer of the Holy Cloak

O Glorious Patriarch St. Joseph, you who were chosen by God above all men to be the earthly head of the most holy of families, we beseech you to accept us within the folds of your holy cloak, that you may become the guardian and custodian of our souls.

From this moment on, we choose you as our father, our protector, our counselor, our patron, and we beseech you to place in your custody our bodies, our souls, all that we are, all that we possess, our lives, and our deaths.

Look upon us as your children; defend us from the treachery of our enemies, invisible or otherwise; assist us at all times in all our necessities; console us in the bitterness of our lives, and especially at the hour of our deaths. Say but one word for us to the Divine Redeemer whom you were deemed worthy to hold in your arms and to the Blessed Virgin Mary, your most chaste spouse. Request for us those blessings that will lead us to salvation. Include us among those who are most dear to you, and we shall set forth to prove ourselves worthy of your special patronage. Amen.

First Wednesdays: Holy Cloak Novena

128.4 Prayer to St. Joseph

To you do we cry in our tribulations, O Blessed Saint Joseph, as we confidently invoke your patronage after that of your most holy spouse, the Blessed Virgin Mary.

By that sacred bond of devotion which linked you to the Immaculate Virgin, Mother of God, and by the fatherly love you lavished on the Child Jesus, we beg you to cast a glance on those heavenly gifts which the Divine Redeemer has obtained for all mankind through His Precious Blood, and through your power and mercy, help us in our needs.

O holy protector of the Holy Family, protect us children of the Lord Jesus Christ; keep far from us the errors and evils which corrupt the world; assist us from Heaven in our struggles against the powers of darkness. And as you once did protect the Divine Child from the cruel edict of Herod, now defend the Church and keep it safe from all dangers and threats; spread over all of us your holy patronage so that by following your example and aided by your spiritual guidance, we may be enabled to lead a holy life, die a happy death, and come at last to the possession of everlasting blessedness in Heaven. Amen.

Praise be to Jesus Christ, now and forever! Amen!

First Fridays

129. A Petition Prayer to the Sacred Heart of Jesus

O Sacred Heart of Jesus, I come to You, throwing myself into the arms of Your tender mercy. You are my sure refuge, my unfailing and only hope. You have a remedy for all my evils, relief for all my miseries, reparation for all my faults. You can supply what is wanting in me in order to obtain fully the graces that I ask for myself and others. You are, for me and for us all, the infallible, inexhaustible source of light, of strength, of perseverance, peace, and consolation. I am certain that my importunity will never weary You; certain, too, that You will never cease to aid, to protect, to love me, because Your love for me, O Divine Heart, is infinite. Have mercy on me then, O Heart of Jesus, and on all that I recommend to You, according to Your own mercy, and do with us, for us, and in us, whatsoever You will, for we abandon ourselves to You with the complete, entire confidence and conviction that You will never abandon us either in time or eternity. Amen

130. Act of Reparation to the Sacred Heart of Jesus

O Heart of Jesus would that we were able to wash away such abominations with our blood. We now offer, in reparation for these violations of Your Divine Honor, the satisfaction You once made to Your Eternal Father on the Cross and which You continue to renew daily on our Altars; we offer it in union with the acts of atonement of Your Virgin Mother and all the Saints and of the pious faithful on earth; and we sincerely promise to make recompense, as far as we can with the help of Your grace, for all neglect of Your great love and for the sins we and other have committed in the past. Amen.

First Fridays

131. Daily Act of Consecration to the Sacred Heart of Jesus

Most Sacred Heart of Jesus, I consecrate myself to Your Most Sacred Heart. Take possession of my whole being; transform me into Yourself. Make my hands, Your hands; my feet, Your feet; my heart, Your heart. Let me see with Your eyes, listen with Your ears, speak with Your lips, love with Your heart, understand with Your mind, serve with Your will, and be dedicated with my whole being. Make me Your other self. Most Sacred Heart of Jesus, send me Your Holy Spirit to teach me to love You and to live through You, with You, in You, and for You.

Come, Holy Spirit, make my body Your temple. Come and abide with me forever. Give me the deepest love for the Sacred Heart of Jesus in order to serve Him with my whole heart, soul, mind, and strength. Take possession of all my faculties of body and soul. Regulate all my passions: feelings and emotions. Take possession of my intellect, understanding, and will; my memory and imagination. O Holy Spirit of Love, give me an abundance of Your efficacious graces. Give me the fullness of all the virtues; enrich my faith, strengthen my hope, increase my trust, and inflame my love.

Give me the fullness of Your sevenfold gifts, fruits, and beatitudes. Most Holy Trinity, make my soul Your sanctuary. Amen.

First Fridays

132. Within Thy Sacred Heart

Within Thy Sacred Heart, I place my every care, dear Lord.

In every need, let me come to Thee with a humble trust, saying, **Heart of Jesus, help me.**
In all my doubts and temptations...
In hours of loneliness, weariness, and trials,...
In the failure of my plans, disappointments, troubles, and sorrows...
When I'm ill, my head and hands cannot work, and I am lonely,...
Always, Always, in spite of weaknesses and falls...
Never forsake me, Heart of Jesus to Thee I cry, grant my petition.
Heart of Jesus, inexhaustible source of love and mercy, give peace to the world. Amen.

133. Sacred Heart Novena Prayer

Heart of Jesus, I give You my heart. I consecrate my entire life to You, and I place in Your hands the eternal disposition of my soul. I ask You for the special grace of uniting myself with Your will so that I might be worthy of receiving Your promises and one day come to share with You in the great joys of Heaven. Amen.

First Fridays

134. Prayer to the Sacred Heart of Jesus-1
by St. Margaret Mary Alacoque

Lord Jesus, let my heart never rest until it finds You, who are its center, its love, and its happiness. By the Wound in Your Heart, pardon the sins that I have committed, whether out of malice or out of evil desires. Place my weak heart in Your own Divine Heart, continually under Your protection and guidance, so that I may persevere in doing good and in fleeing evil until my last breath. Amen.

135. Prayer to the Sacred Heart of Jesus-2

O Most holy Heart of Jesus, fountain of every blessing. I adore Thee, I love Thee, and with a lively sorrow for my sins, I offer Thee this poor heart of mine. Make me humble, patient, pure, and wholly obedient to Thy will. Grant, good Jesus that I may live in Thee and for Thee, protect me in the midst of danger, comfort me in my afflictions, and give me health of body assistance in my temporal needs. Thy blessing on all that I do, and the grace of a holy death. Within Thy Heart, I place my every care. In every need, let me come to Thee with humble trust, saying, Heart of Jesus, help me. Amen.

First Fridays

136. Invocations to the Sacred Heart

Merciful Jesus, I consecrate myself today and always to Thy Most Sacred Heart. Most Sacred Heart of Jesus, I implore, that I may ever love Thee more and more. Most Sacred Heart of Jesus, I Trust in Thee. Most Sacred Heart of Jesus, have mercy on us. Sacred Heart of Jesus, I believe in Thy love for me. Jesus, meek and humble of heart, make my heart like unto Thine. Sacred Heart of Jesus, Thy Kingdom come. Most Sacred Heart of Jesus convert sinners, save the dying, and deliver the Holy Souls from Purgatory. Amen.

First Saturdays

137. Act of Reparation to the Immaculate Heart of Mary

Most Holy Virgin Mother, we listen with grief to the complaints of your Immaculate Heart surrounded with the thorns placed therein at every moment by the blasphemies and ingratitude of ungrateful humanity. We are moved by the ardent desire of loving you as Our Mother and of promoting a true devotion to your Immaculate Heart.

We, therefore, kneel before you to manifest the sorrow we feel for the grievances that people cause you and to atone by our prayers and sacrifices for the offenses with which they return your love. Obtain for them and for us the pardon of so many sins. Hasten the conversion of sinners that they may love Jesus and cease to offend the Lord, already so much offended. Turn your eyes of mercy toward us, that we may love God with all our heart on earth and enjoy Him forever in Heaven. Amen.

First Saturday

138. Prayer to the Sacred Heart of Jesus & the Immaculate Heart of Mary-1

O Blessed Mother, I renew and ratify today in thy hands the vows of my Baptism; I renounce forever Satan, his pomps and works; and I give myself entirely to Jesus Christ, the Incarnate Wisdom, to carry my cross after Him all the days of my life, and to be more faithful to Him than I have ever been before. In the presence of all the heavenly court, I choose thee this day for my Mother and Mistress. I deliver and consecrate to thee, as thy slave, my body and soul, my goods, both interior and exterior, and even the value of all my good actions, past, present, and future, leaving to thee the entire and full right of disposing of me, and all that belongs to me, without exception, according to thy good pleasure, for the greater glory of God in time and in eternity.

O, Mary, conceived without sin, pray for us who have recourse to thee. Amen.

First Saturday

139. Prayer to the Sacred Heart of Jesus & the Immaculate Heart of Mary-2

Most Sacred Heart of Jesus, truly present in the Holy Eucharist, I consecrate my body and soul to be entirely one with Your heart, being sacrificed at every instant on all the altars of the world and giving praise to the Father, pleading for the coming of His Kingdom. Please receive this humble offering of myself. Use me as You will for the glory of the Father and the salvation of souls.

Queen of the Most Holy Rosary and tender Mother of all people, I consecrate myself to your Immaculate Heart and recommend to you my family, my country, and the whole human race. Please accept my consecration, dearest Mother, and use me as you wish to accomplish your designs upon the world. O Immaculate Heart of Mary, Queen of Heaven and earth, rule over me and teach me how to allow the Heart of Jesus to rule and triumph in me and around me, as it has ruled and triumphed in you. Amen.

Sacred Heart of Jesus, Immaculate Heart of Mary, Most Chaste Heart of St. Joseph, protect us!

Heavenly Father, through the Holy Spirit, we offer You all for the Sacred Eucharistic Heart of Jesus, all through the Immaculate Heart of Mary, all in union with the Most Chaste Heart of St. Joseph! Amen.

January

Month of the Holy Name of Jesus

140. Praise You Jesus

Praise You, Jesus, You are my Life, my Love.
Praise You, Jesus, You are the Lord of lords.
Praise You, Jesus, You are Christ, the King.
Praise You, Jesus, You are the Light of the World.
Praise You, Jesus, You are the Way for our Life.
Praise You, Jesus, You are the only Truth.
Praise You, Jesus, You are the Prince of Peace.
Praise You, Jesus, You are the Living Word.
Praise You, Jesus, You are the Messiah.
Praise You, Jesus, You are the Good Shepherd.
Praise You, Jesus, You are the Rock of all ages.
Praise You, Jesus, You are our Fortress.
Praise You, Jesus, You are our Victory.
Praise You, Jesus, You are our Salvation.
Praise You, Jesus, You are our Wisdom.
Praise You, Jesus, You are the Great "I AM".
Praise You, Jesus, You are our Joy.
Praise You, Jesus, You are my Defense.
Praise You, Jesus, You are my Protector.
Praise You, Jesus, You are all that I need.
Praise You, Jesus, You are all that I want.
Praise You, Jesus, You are our Strength.
Praise You, Jesus, You are the Almighty.
Praise You, Jesus, You are the Alpha and the Omega.
Praise You, Jesus, You are the Savior of the World.

January: Month of the Holy Name of Jesus
141. Veni, Creator Spiritus
Plenary Indulgence: Jan 1

Come, Holy Spirit, Creator blest, and in our souls take up Thy rest; come with Thy grace and heavenly aid to fill the hearts which Thou hast made.

O Comforter, to Thee we cry, O Heavenly Gift of God Most High, O Fount of Life and Fire of Love, and Sweet Anointing from above.

Thou in Thy sevenfold gifts are known; Thou, finger of God's hand we own; Thou, promise of the Father, Thou Who dost the tongue with power imbue.

Kindle our sense from above, and make our hearts o'erflow with love; with patience firm and virtue high the weakness of our flesh supply.

Far from us drive the foe we dread, and grant us Thy peace instead; so shall we not, with Thee for guide, turn from the path of life aside.

Oh, may Thy grace on us bestow the Father and the Son to know; and Thee, through endless times confessed, of both the eternal Spirit blest.

Now to the Father and the Son, Who rose from death, be glory given, with Thou, O Holy Comforter, henceforth by all in earth and heaven. Amen.

January: Month of the Holy Name of Jesus

142. Epiphany Home Blessing

Traditionally, Catholics bless their home and those who live in their household on the Feast of the Epiphany each year. It's not difficult to do, and we highly recommend you give it a try! Here's how.

Write on your door frame: **20 + C + M + B + (year)**

The letters C, M, and B have two meanings. They are the initials of the traditional names of the three magi: Caspar, Melchior, and Balthazar. They also represent the Latin words "Christus Mansionem Benedicat," which means "May Christ bless the house." The "+" signs symbolize the cross, and the beginning and the last digits represent the year, i.e., 2023.

What You'll Need To Bless Your Home On The Epiphany
Prayers   Chalk   A doorway   A ladder or chair.

143. Prayers for the Epiphany Home Blessing

Feast Day: Jan 6

Lord God of Heaven and earth, You revealed Your only-begotten Son to every nation by the guidance of a star. Bless this house and all who inhabit it. Fill them (us) with the light of Christ, that their (our) concern for others may reflect Your love. We ask this through Christ our Lord. Amen

The leader concludes the rite by signing himself or herself with the sign of the cross and saying:

May Christ Jesus dwell with us, keep us from all harm, and make us one in mind and heart, now and forever. Amen.

January: Month of the Holy Name of Jesus

144. Prayer to St. Sebastian

Feast Day: Jan 20

Glorious Sebastian, martyr, and Saint, I call on your strength and courage to help me through this difficult trial. Your faith was so deep that a multitude of arrows could not finish you. The piercing wounds inflicted for your faith only proved to strengthen your belief. May you intercede for those who are weakened from the effects of disease. I ask for your intercession that I may also survive that which threatens to destroy my belief in the mercy of Christ. Amen

145. Novena to Our Lady Good Success

Begin: Jan 24 *Feast Day: Feb 1*

Our Lady of Good Success, we know that you are always ready to hear our cries and soothe our pain. We know that you are powerful in obtaining mercy for sinners, so we turn to you in confidence. When you appeared to Mother Mariana, you spoke often about the state of the Church and the many tribulations the Church would face in the future. As you spoke of these evils, you said that prayer and self-denial were necessary to combat them.

In your apparitions as Our Lady of Good Success, you came to us as a Mother, always ready to ask your Son for aid on our behalf. Please bring my petitions before the throne of Christ! Heavenly Queen, you desire peace and holiness for all of us and for the Church established by your Son. We beg you to make use of your heavenly influence to obtain graces for the Church today. And I also ask you to present my particular requests before your Son: *(mention here)*.

Our Lady of Good Success, pray for us. Amen.

January: Month of the Holy Name of Jesus

146. St. Don Bosco's Prayer to Mary

Feast Day: Jan 31

Most Holy Virgin Mary, Help of Christians, how sweet it is to come to your feet imploring your perpetual help. If earthly mothers cease not to remember their children, how can you, the most loving of all mothers, forget me?

Grant then to me, I implore you, your perpetual help in all my necessities, in every sorrow, and especially in all my temptations. I ask for your unceasing help for all who are now suffering. Help the weak, cure the sick, convert sinners. Grant through your intercessions many vocations to the religious life. Obtain for us, O Mary, Help of Christians, that having invoked you on earth, we may love and eternally thank you in heaven. Amen.

February

Month of the Holy Family

147. Feast of the Presentation Prayer

Feast Day: Feb 2

Almighty and Ever-Living God, as Your only-begotten Son was this day presented in the temple in the substance of our flesh, grant that we may be presented to You with pure and clean hearts through Jesus Christ, our Lord, who lives and reigns with You and the Holy Spirit, one God, now and forever. Amen.

148. Consecration to the Flame of Holy Love

Feast Day: Feb 2

O Immaculate Heart of Mary, humbly, I ask that you take my heart into the Flame of Holy Love, that is the spiritual refuge of all mankind. Do not look upon my faults and failings, but allow these iniquities to be burned away by this purifying Flame. Through Holy Love, help me to be sanctified in the present moment, and in so doing, give to you, dear Mother, my every thought, word, and action. Take me and use me according to your great pleasure. Allow me to be your instrument in the world, all for the greater glory of God, towards your victorious reign. Amen.

149. St. Blaise Intercession

Feast Day: Feb 3

Through the intercession of St. Blaise, bishop, and martyr, may God deliver you from every disease of the throat and from every other illness. In the Name of the Father, and of the Son, and of the Holy Spirit **(+)**. Amen.

February: Month of the Holy Family

150. Flame of Love Rosary

This version of the rosary was revealed to Elizabth Kindelmann, a poor and humble mystic from Hungary and a Third-Order Carmelite. It is approved by the Church and was given by Jesus and Mary specifically with the purpose of blinding Satan so that he loses his influence over families, communities, and all people.

Opening & Concluding Prayer:

We offer ourselves to the heavenly Father through all the wounds of Our Saviour Jesus Christ.
We kiss the wound of your Sacred Left Hand with sorrow deep and true. **(+)**
We kiss the wound of your Sacred Right Hand with sorrow deep and true. **(+)**
We kiss the wound of your Sacred Left Foot with sorrow deep and true. **(+)**
We kiss the wound of your Sacred Right foot with sorrow deep and true. **(+)**
We kiss the wound of your Sacred Side with sorrow deep and true. **(+)**

Continue the format of the normal rosary, except Hail Mary beads have an alternate Hail Mary prayer.

Hail Mary:

Hail Mary, full of grace, the Lord is with thee. Blessed art thou among women, and blessed is the fruit of thy womb, Jesus.
Holy Mary, Mother of God, pray for us sinners, **spread the effect of grace of thy Flame of Love over all of humanity, now and at the hour of our death.** Amen.

Prayer After Each Decade:

Come Holy Spirit, come by the means of The Power of thy Flame of Love of the Immaculate Heart of Mary. Amen.

Additional Prayers:

~My Adorable Jesus -We ask You to take us in Spirit before the Eucharistic Presence throughout the world. Amen.
~Blessed Lady - Take us and place us where we belong in the Divine Fire. Share with us your Immaculate Conception. Amen.

February: Month of the Holy Family

151. Novena to Our Lady of Lourdes

Begin: Feb 2 *Feast Day: Feb 11*

O glorious Mother of God, so powerful under your special title of Our Lady of Lourdes, to you we raise our hearts and hands to implore your powerful intercession in obtaining from the Gracious Heart of Jesus all the helps and graces necessary for our spiritual and temporal welfare and for the special favor we so earnestly seek.

**Our Lady of Lourdes, pray for us.
Saint Bernadette, pray for us. Amen.**

February: Month of the Holy Family

152. The Holy Face Novena

Begin: 9 days prior to Fat Tuesday *Feast Day: Fat Tuesday*

Eternal Father, we offer You the Holy Face of Jesus, covered with blood, sweat, dust, and spittle, in reparation for our sins and the sins of the whole world.

Eternal Father, I offer Thee the Adorable Face of Thy Beloved Son, for the honor and glory of Thy Holy Name, for the conversion of sinners, and for the salvation of the dying. Amen.

153. Prayer to the Holy Face of Jesus

O Blessed Face of my kind Savior, by the tender love and piercing sorrow of Our Lady as she beheld You in Your cruel Passion, grant us to share in this intense sorrow and love so as to fulfill the Holy Will of God to the utmost of our ability. Amen.

154. Offering of the Holy Face of Our Lord Jesus Christ to God the Father

Eternal Father, turn away Your angry gaze from our guilty people whose face has become unsightly in Your eyes. Look instead upon the Face of Your Beloved Son, in Whom You are well pleased. We now offer You this Holy Face, covered with shame and disfigured by bloody bruises, in reparation for the crimes of our age, in order to appease Your anger, justly provoked against us. Because Your Divine Son, our Redeemer, had taken upon His Head all the sins of His members, that they might be spared, we now beg You, Eternal Father, to grant us mercy. Amen

O Bleeding Face, O Face Divine, be every adoration Thine. *(3x)*

Lent

155. Prayer to Jesus Christ Crucified

My Good and Dear Jesus, I kneel before You, asking You most earnestly to engrave upon my heart a deep and lively faith, hope, and charity, with true repentance for my sins and a firm resolve to make amends. As I reflect upon Your five Wounds and dwell upon them with deep compassion and grief, I recall, Good Jesus, the words the prophet David spoke long ago concerning Yourself: "They have pierced my hands and my feet; they have counted all my bones!" Amen.

156. Fatima Prayer- Reparation

Most Holy Trinity, Father, Son, and Holy Spirit (+), I adore Thee profoundly. I offer Thee the Most Precious Body, Blood, Soul, and Divinity of Jesus Christ, present in all the tabernacles of the world, in reparation for the outrages, sacrileges, and indifferences whereby He is offended. And through the infinite merits of His Most Sacred Heart and the Immaculate Heart of Mary, I beg of Thee the conversion of poor sinners. Amen.

Lent

157. Prayer to the Holy Face of Jesus- Reparation

Almighty and Eternal Father, since it has pleased Our Divine Savior to reveal to mankind in modern times the power residing in His Holy Face, we now avail ourselves of this treasure in our great need. Since our Savior Himself promised that by offering to You His Holy Face disfigured in the Passion, we can procure the settlement of all the affairs of our household and that nothing whatsoever will be refused to us, we now come before Your Throne.

Eternal Father, turn away Your angry gaze from our guilty people whose face has become unsightly in Your eyes. Look instead upon the Face of Your Beloved Son; for this is the Face of Him in whom You are well pleased. We now offer You His Holy Face covered with blood, sweat, dust, spittle, and exhaustion in reparation for the worst crimes of our age, which are atheism, blasphemy, impurity, immodesty, apostasy in Your Holy Church, and the desecration of Your holy days. We thus hope to appease Your anger justly provoked against us. The All-Merciful Advocate opens His mouth to plead our cause; listen to His cries, behold His tears, O God, and through the merits of His Holy Face, hearken to Him when He intercedes for us poor miserable sinners. Amen.

158. Act of Consecration to the Holy Face of Jesus

O Lord Jesus, we believe most firmly in You; we love You. You are the Eternal Son of God and the Son Incarnate of the Blessed Virgin Mary. You are the Lord and Absolute Ruler of all creation. We acknowledge You, therefore, as the Universal Sovereign of all creatures. You are the Lord and Supreme Ruler of all mankind, and we, in acknowledging Your dominion, consecrate ourselves to You now and forever. Loving Jesus, we place our family under the protection of Your Holy Face and of Your Virgin Mother Mary, most sorrowful. We promise to be faithful to You for the rest of our lives and to observe with fidelity Your Holy Commandments. We will never deny before men You and Your Divine rights over us and all mankind. Grant us the grace to never sin again; nevertheless, should we fail, O Divine Savior, have mercy on us and restore us to Your grace. Radiate Your Divine Countenance upon us and bless us now and forever. Embrace us at the hour of our death in Your Kingdom for all eternity, through the intercession of Your Blessed Mother, of all Your Saints who behold You in Heaven, and the just who glorify You on earth. O Jesus, be mindful of us forever and never forsake us; protect our family. O Mother of Sorrows, by the eternal glory which you enjoy in Heaven, through the merits of your bitter anguish in the Sacred Passion of your Beloved Son, our Lord Jesus Christ, obtain for us the grace that the Precious Blood shed by Jesus for the redemption of our souls, be not shed for us in vain. We love you, O Mary. Embrace us and bless us, O Mother. Protect us in life and in death. Amen.

Glory be.... Amen.

159. Prayers of the Passion- Mother of Sorrows

O Mother of Sorrows, by the anguish and love with which thou did stand at the Cross of Jesus, stand by me in my last agony. To thy maternal heart, I commend the last three hours of my life. Offer these hours to the Eternal Father in union with the agony of our dearest Lord, in atonement for my sins. Offer to the Eternal Father the Most Precious Blood of Jesus, mingled with your tears on Calvary, that I may obtain the grace of receiving Holy Communion with the most perfect love and contrition before my death and that I may breathe forth my soul in the adorable presence of Jesus. Dearest Mother, when the moment of my death has at last come, present me as your child to Jesus. Ask Him to forgive me for having offended Him, for I knew not what I did. Beg Him to receive me into His kingdom of glory to be united with Him forever. Amen

March

Month of the St. Joseph

160. Petition for St. Jospeh's Blessing

Bless me, O dearly beloved father, St. Joseph; bless my body and soul; bless my resolutions, my words, and deeds, all that I possess, all my interior and exterior goods, that all may redound to the greater honor of God. Bless me for time and eternity, and preserve me from every sin.

Obtain for me the grace to make atonement for all my sins by love and contrition here on earth, so that after my last breath I may, without delay, prostrated at your feet, returning thanks in Heaven for all the love and goodness You, O ddearestfather, have shown me here below. Amen.

161. Act of Consecration to St. Joseph

O dearest Saint Joseph, I consecrate myself to your honor and give myself to you that you may always be my father, my protector, and my guide in the way of salvation. Obtain for me a greater purity of heart and fervent love of the interior life. After your example, may I do all my actions for the greater glory of God, in union with the Divine Heart of Jesus and the Immaculate Heart of Mary. O Blessed Saint Joseph, pray for me, that I may share in the peace and joy of your holy death. Amen.

March: Month of the St. Joseph

162. Breastplate Prayer of St. Patrick
Shortened Version

Feast Day: March 17

Christ with me, Christ before me, Christ behind me, Christ in me, Christ beneath me, Christ above me, Christ on my right, Christ on my left, Christ when I lie down, Christ when I sit down, Christ when I arise, Christ in the heart of every man who thinks of me, Christ in the mouth of everyone who speaks of me, Christ in every eye that sees me, Christ in every ear that hears me. Amen.

163. Good St. Joseph

O St. Joseph, you did everything out of love for Jesus and Mary; help us to do the same. You are the Parton Saint of interior life, please attain for us that precious gift of perpetual prayer from the heart. O St. Joseph, Terror of Demons, protect us, our loved ones, and our Rosary Family from all attacks of the devil. Amen.

March: Month of the St. Joseph

164. Novena to St. Joseph

Begin: March 11 *Feast Day: March 19*

O Glorious St. Joseph, faithful follower of Jesus Christ, to thee do we raise our hearts and hands to implore thy powerful intercession in obtaining from the Good Heart of Jesus all the helps and graces necessary for our spiritual and temporal welfare, particularly the grace of happy death, and the special favor we now implore *(mention here)*.

O guardian of the Word Incarnate, we feel animated with confidence that thy prayers on our behalf will be graciously heard before the throne of God.

(the following bold are is to be said seven times in honor of the seven joys or sorrows of St. Joseph)

O glorious St. Joseph, through the love thou dost bear to Jesus Christ and for the glory of His name, hear our prayers and obtain our petitions. *(7x)*

Let us pray: O Glorious St. Joseph, spouse of the Immaculate Virgin, obtain for me a pure, humble, and charitable mind and perfect resignation to the Divine Will. Be my guide, father, and model through life, that I may merit to die as thou didst in the arms of Jesus and Mary. St. Joseph, friend of the Sacred Heart, pray for us. Amen.

Divine Mercy Sunday

165. Our Lady of Mercy Prayer

Mary, Mother of God, I turn to you in all my pressing needs and difficulties as to a most sure refuge. I implore the help of your protection and choose you as my advocate. I entrust my cause to you, who is the Mother of Mercy, and I wish to offer you day by day my most reverent love. But that my devotion may be pleasing to you, help me to maintain my soul and body in the spotlessness of your purity, help me to try as best I can to walk in your footsteps, humbly seeking to be like you. Even if I have committed all possible sins, let me never lose confidence in you, for I know I shall always find your Heart filled with mercy. The Son of God has His justice, but you, the Mother, have only your mercy. You desire more to do good to me than I can desire to receive favors from you, for your Heart is all love and mercy. Mary, My Mother, how shall I stand before my Judge at the day of judgment? How shall I answer for the wasted days and years that God has given me to serve Him alone? I look to you, Mother of Mercy. You are all-merciful that you may obtain for me pardon and mercy. You are kind and loving, for you have a mother's Heart, full of pity for the erring. You are a Mother of Mercy to the sinner and the fallen; have pity on me! Amen.

April

Month of the Blessed Sacrament

166. Come Reign In Me

Jesus, I believe You are the Son of God. I believe that You died on the Cross to rescue me from sin and death and to restore me to the Father. I believe that You are present in every Tabernacle throughout the world. That You did not abandon me. I believe that You chose to come in a Tiny Host, so small and humble, as when You were an infant. Hidden from me, but ever-present, ever-powerful, ever-merciful, and ready at any moment to welcome me. You chose me.

Today, I choose to turn from my sins, my self-centeredness, and every part of my life that does not please You. Today, I choose You. I give myself to You. I receive Your forgiveness and ask You to take Your rightful place in my life as my Savior and Lord. Come reign in my heart, fill me with Your love and Your life, and help me become a truly loving person like You. Restore me, Jesus. Live in me. Love through me. Let Your rays of love pierce and flood the souls of every member of my family, every friend and neighbor.

O Jesus, with Your Power and Your Mercy, cast out all depression, addiction, brokenness, trauma, fear, anxiety, worry, confusion, hatred, impurity, unforgiveness, and hopelessness. Cover me and my loved ones with Your Precious Blood. By Your Precious Blood, heal us, transform us, make our hearts like unto Yours. In Jesus' Name, I pray. Amen.

April: Month of the Blessed Sacrament

167. Novena to Our Lady of Good Counsel

Begin: April 17 *Feast Day: April 26*

O Holy Virgin, to whose feet we are led by our anxious uncertainty in our search for and attainment of what is true and good, invoking you by the sweet title of Mother of Good Counsel, we beseech you to come to our assistance when, along the road of this life, the darkness of error and of evil conspires towards our ruin by leading our minds and our hearts astray.

O Seat of Wisdom and Star of the Sea, enlighten the doubtful and the erring, that they may not be seduced by the false appearances of good; render them steadfast in the face of the hostile and corrupting influences of passion and of sin.

O Mother of Good Counsel, obtain for us from your Divine Son a great love of virtue, and, in the hour of uncertainty and trial, the strength to embrace the way that leads to our salvation.

If your hand sustains us, we shall walk unmolested along the path indicated to us by the life and words of Jesus, our Redeemer, and having followed freely and securely, even in the midst of this world's strife, the Sun of Truth and Justice under your maternal Star, we shall come to the enjoyment of full and eternal peace with you in the haven of salvation. Amen.

We pray especially for the intention in this novena of *(mention here)*.
Pray an Our Father, Hail Mary & Glory Be

Our Lady of Good Counsel, pray for us! Amen.

168. Prayer to Our Lady of Good Counsel

Feast Day: April 26

We turn to you, Our Mother of Good Counsel, as we seek to imitate your faith-filled life. May we be led by the same Wisdom which God sent forth from heaven to guide you along unfamiliar paths and through challenging decisions. Keep us united in mind and heart as we go forward in joyful hope toward the grace-filled freedom that St. Augustine recommends. O Virgin Mother of Good Counsel, hear our prayer as we look to you for guidance. Pray for us to our Loving and Merciful Father, to Your Son, our Lord Jesus Christ, and to the Holy Spirit, Giver of All Wisdom, One God, forever and ever. Amen.

May

Month of the Blessed Virgin Mary

169. Short Prayer of Reparation to the Virgin Mary

O Blessed Virgin, Mother of God, look down in mercy from Heaven, where you are enthroned as Queen, upon me, a miserable sinner, your unworthy servant. Although I know full well my own unworthiness, yet in order to atone for the offenses that are done to you by impious and blasphemous tongues, from the depths of my heart, I praise and extol you as the purest, the fairest, the holiest creature of all God's handiwork. I bless your Holy name; I praise your exalted privilege of being truly Mother of God, ever-Virgin, conceived without stain of sin, Co-Redemptrix of the human race. I bless the Eternal Father who specially chose you for His daughter; I bless the Word Incarnate who took upon Himself our nature in your bosom and made you His Mother; I bless the Holy Spirit who took you as His bride. All honor, praise, and thanksgiving to the ever-blessed Trinity who predestined you and loved you so exceedingly from all eternity as to exalt thee above all creatures to the most sublime heights. O Virgin, holy and merciful, obtain for all who offend thee the grace of repentance, and graciously accept this poor act of homage from me, your servant, obtaining likewise for me from your Divine Son the pardon and remission of all my sins. Amen.

170. Novena to St. Dymphna

Begin: May 6 *Feast Day: May 15*

Lord, our God, you graciously chose St. Dymphna as patroness of those afflicted with mental, emotional, and nervous disorders. She is thus an inspiration and a symbol of charity to the thousands who ask for her intercession.

Please grant, Lord, through the prayers of this pure, youthful martyr, relief and consolation to all suffering such trials, especially those for whom we pray *(mention here)*.

We beg You, Lord, to hear the prayers of St. Dymphna on our behalf. Grant all those for whom we pray patience in their sufferings and resignation to Your Divine Will. Please fill them with hope and grant them the relief and cure they so much desire. We ask this through Christ our Lord, who suffered agony in the Garden. Amen.

171. Prayer to St. Rita for Impossible Cases & Special Needs

Feast Day: May 22

Holy Patroness of those in need, St. Rita, so humble, pure, and patient, whose pleadings with thy Divine Spouse are irresistible, obtain for me from thy Crucified Christ my request (mention here). Be kind to me for the greater glory of God, and I promise to honor thee and to sing thy praises forever.

Oh, glorious St. Rita, who didst miraculously participate in the sorrowful Passion of our Lord Jesus Christ, obtain for me the grace to suffer with resignation the troubles of this life and protect me in all my needs. Amen.

172. Prayer to St. Joan of Arc

Feast Day: May 30

Most extraordinary soldier, you insistently proclaim, "Let God be served first!" You began by winning many victories and received the praises of princes, but then you were given to the enemy and cruely put to death. Instill in us the desire to serve God first and perform our earthly tasks with that idea ever in our minds. In Jesus' Name, we pray. Amen

Pentecost

173. Consecration to the Holy Spirit

O Holy Spirit, receive the perfect and absolute consecration of all my being. Deign that from now on, in every moment of my life and in all of my actions, be my Director and all the love of my heart. I abandon myself without reserve to your Divine Action and wish to be ever docile to Your inspirations. O Holy Spirit, transform me with Mary and in Mary into Christ Jesus for the Glory of the Father and the salvation of the world. Amen.

174. Daily Consecration to the Holy Spirit

O Most Holy Spirit, receive the consecration that I make of my entire being. From this moment on, come into every area of my life and into each of my actions. Thou art my Light, my Guide, my Strength, and the sole desire of my heart. I abandon myself without reserve to Thy Divine Action, and I desire to be ever docile to Thine inspirations. O Holy Spirit, transform me with and through Mary into "another Christ Jesus" for the Glory of the Father and the salvation of the world. Amen

175. Ablaze with the Fire of Your Spirit

O Lord, have mercy on us, take away from me my sins, and mercifully set me ablaze with the Fire of Your Holy Spirit. Take away from me the heart of stone, and give me a human heart, a heart to love and adore You, a heart to delight in You, and to courageously follow You! Amen.

Pentecost
176. Novena Holy Spirit

Begin: Friday after Ascension Thursday *Feast Day: Pentecost*

On my knees, before the great cloud of heavenly witnesses, I offer myself body and soul to Thee, Eternal Spirit of God. I adore the brightness of Thy Purity, the unerring keenness of Thy Justice, and the might of Thy Love. Thou art the strength and light of my soul. In Thee, I live and move and have my being. I desire never to grieve Thee by unfaithfulness to grace, and I pray with all my Heart to be kept from the smallest sin against Thee. Make me faithful in every thought, and grant that I may always listen to Thy Voice, watch for Thy Light, and follow Thy Gracious Inspirations. I cling to Thee and give myself to Thee, and I ask Thee by Thy compassion to watch over me in my weakness. Holding the Pierced Feet of Jesus, looking at His five Wounds, trusting in His Precious Blood and adoring His Opened Side and stricken Heart, I implore Thee, adorable Spirit, Helper of my infirmity, so to keep me in Thy grace that I may never sin against Thee with the sin which Thou wilt not forgive. Grant to me the grace, O Holy Spirit, Spirit of the Father and of the Son, to say to Thee always and everywhere, "Speak, Lord, for Thy servant hears." Amen.

177. Prayer for the Seven Gifts of the Holy Spirit

O Lord Jesus Christ Who, before ascending into heaven, did promise to send the Holy Spirit to finish Your work in the souls of Your Apostles and Disciples, Deign to grant the same Holy Spirit to me that He may perfect in my soul, the work of Your Grace and Your Love. Grant me the Spirit of Wisdom that I may despise the perishable things of this world and aspire only after the things that are eternal, the Spirit of Understanding to enlighten my mind with the light of Your Divine Truth, the Spirit of Counsel that I may ever choose the surest way of pleasing God and gaining heaven, the Spirit of Fortitude that I may bear my cross with You and that I may overcome with courage all the obstacles that oppose my salvation, the Spirit of Knowledge that I may know God and know myself and grow perfect in the science of the Saints, the Spirit of Piety that I may find the service of God sweet and amiable, and the Spirit of Fear that I may be filled with a loving reverence towards God and may dread in any way to displease Him. Mark me, dear Lord, with the sign of Your true disciples, and animate me in all things with Your Spirit. Amen.

Pentecost

178. Prayer to the Indwelling Most Holy Trinity

Solemnity: Sunday after Pentecost

O my Love, my only Good, Most Holy Trinity, I adore You, hidden in the depths of my soul. To You, to Your honor and glory, I dedicate my life. May every thought, word, and deed of mine be an act of adoration and praise directed towards Your Divine Majesty enthroned in my heart.

O Father, Infinite Goodness, behold Your child, clothed in the likeness of Your Son. Extend to me Your arms that I may belong to You forever.
O Son, Divine Lord, made man, crucify me with Yourself that I may become, in union with You, a sacrifice of praise for the glory of Your Father.

O Holy Spirit, Fire of Everlasting Love, consume me on the altar of Divine Charity, that at the end of life, nothing may remain but that which bears the likeness of Christ.

O Blessed Trinity, worthy of all adoration, I wish to remain in spirit on my knees, to acknowledge forever Your reign in me and over me, to Your everlasting glory.

Through the Immaculate Heart of Mary and the pure heart of St. Joseph, I consecrate my life to Your adoration and glory.
At the moment of death, receive me, O my Triune Love, that I may continue my adoration of love through all eternity. Amen.

Pentecost

179. Act of Consecration to Our Lady of the Blessed Trinity

Solemity: Sunday after Pentecost

With all my heart, I praise you, Most Holy Virgin, above all Angels and Saints in Paradise, Daughter of the Eternal Father, and I consecrate to you my soul with all its faculties.

Hail Mary...

With all my heart, I praise you, Most Holy Virgin, above all Angels and Saints in Paradise, beloved Mother of the Son of God. I consecrate to you my body with all its senses.
Hail Mary...

With all my heart, I praise you, Most Holy Virgin, about all Angels and Saints in Paradise, beloved Spouse of the Holy Spirit. I consecrate to you my heart with all its affections and beseech you to obtain for me from the Most Holy Trinity all the graces necessary for salvation.

Hail Mary...

June

Month of the Most Sacred Heart of Jesus

180. An Act of Consecration to the Sacred Heart of Jesus

Most Sacred Heart of Jesus, I wish to live in You, in Your grace, in which I desire at all costs to preserve. Keep me from sin and strengthen my will by helping me to keep watch over my senses, my imagination, and my heart. Help me to correct my faults, which are the source of sin. I beg You to do this, O Jesus, through Mary, Your Immaculate Mother. Amen.

181. Sacred Heart of Jesus

Sacred Heart of Jesus, filled with infinite love, broken by my ingratitude, pierced by my sins, yet loving me still, accept the consecration that I make to You, of all that I am and all that I have. Take every faculty of my soul and body, and draw me, day by day, nearer and nearer to Your Sacred Side, and there, as I can bear the lesson, teach me Your blessed ways. Amen.

182. Sacred Heart of Jesus Consecration

Most Sacred Heart of Jesus, through the Immaculate Heart of Your loving Mother, I consecrate myself to You in union with the Holy Sacrifice of the Mass. Transform my heart, bestow Your thoughts, Your will, Your love, to be Your life. Jesus, take possession of my whole being that You may love the Father through me, with me, and in me, for You are my Lord and Savior. Amen.

See Additional Prayers to the Sacred Heart in First Friday Devotions

June: Month of the Most Sacred Heart of Jesus

183. Mother of Perpetual Help, For Graces & Salvation

Feast Day: June 27

O Mother of Perpetual Help, you are the dispenser of all the goods which God grants to us miserable sinners, and for this reason, He has made you so powerful, so rich, and so bountiful that you may help us in our misery.

Come then, to my aid, dearest Mother, for I recommend myself to you. In your hands, I place my soul. Count me among your most devoted servants; take me under your protection, and it is enough for me. For if you protect me, dear Mother, I fear nothing: not from my sins, because you will obtain for me the pardon of them; not from the devils, because you are more powerful than all hell together; nor even from Jesus, my Judge Himself, because by one prayer from you, He will be appeased.

But one thing I fear is that in the hour of temptation, I may neglect to call on you and thus perish miserably. Obtain for me, then the pardon of my sins, love for Jesus, final perseverance, and the grace always to have recourse to you, O Mother of Perpetual Help.

Hail Mary (3x)

184. Mother of Perpetual Help

Feast Day: June 27

O Mother of Perpetual Help, grant that I may ever invoke your most powerful name, which is the safeguard of the living and the salvation of the dying... But I will not be content with merely pronouncing your name: let my love for you prompt me ever to hail you, Mother of Perpetual Help. Amen.

June: Month of the Most Sacred Heart of Jesus

185. Prayer to Sts. Peter and Paul for the Holy Catholic Church

Feast Day: June 29

Defend, O Lord, Your servants, we beseech You, from all dangers both of body and soul; and, by the intercession of the blessed and glorious Virgin Mary, Mother of God, of the blessed Apostles Peter and Paul, and of all Your Saints, mercifully grant us the blessings of peace and safety; that all adversities and errors being removed, the Church may freely and securely serve You; through Christ Our Lord. Amen.

July

Month of the Precious Blood of Jesus Christ

186. Prayer for Calling on the Precious Blood of Our Lord

Heavenly Father, in the name of Jesus Thy Son, I pray: May the Precious Blood of Jesus wash over me and through me. Let it heal any and every wound and scar so that the devil may find no place in me. Cause it to saturate and fill up my whole being: my heart, soul, mind, and body; my memory and my imagination; my past and my present; every fiber of my being, every molecule, every atom. Let there remain no part of me untouched by His Precious Blood. Make it flow over and around the altar of my heart on every side. Fill and heal, especially the wounds and scars of/caused by *(mention here)*. These things I ask of You, Heavenly Father, in the name of Jesus through Mary's intercession. Amen.

187. Prayer to the Precious Blood

Eternal Father, I offer Thee the Precious Blood of Jesus Christ, the merits, love, and sufferings of His Sacred Heart, the tears and sorrows of our Immaculate Mother, as the price of the favor I wish to obtain if it is for Thy Glory and my salvation. Amen.

July: Month of the Precious Blood of Jesus Christ

188. Our Lady, The Immaculate Conception
Patroness of the United States of America since 1847

July 4

God our Father, Giver of Life, we entrust the United States of America to Your loving care. You are the rock on which this nation was founded. You alone are the true source of our cherished rights to life, liberty, and the pursuit of happiness. Reclaim this land for Your glory and dwell among Your people. Send Your Spirit to touch the hearts of our nation's leaders. Open their minds to the beauty of marriage between a man and woman and the great dignity of human life at all ages. Remind Your people that true happiness is rooted in seeking and doing Your will. Through the intercession of Mary Immaculate, the Patroness of our land grant us the courage to be one nation under God truly. Amen.

189. Miracle Prayer to St. Benedict

Feast Day: July 11

Admirable Saint and Doctor of humility, you practiced what you taught, assiduously praying for God's glory and lovingly fulfilling all work for God and the benefit of all human beings. You know the many physical dangers that surround us today, often caused or occasioned by human inventions. Guard us against poisoning of the body as well as of mind and soul, and thus be truly a "Blessed one for us." Amen.

190. St. Sharbel Intercession Prayer

Feast Day: July 24

O Lord, infinitely holy and glorified in your Saints, you inspired the holy monk and hermit St. Sharbel to live and die in the way of Jesus Christ. You gave him the strength to detach himself from the world in order to make the monastic virtues triumph in his hermitage.

We implore you to bestow upon us the grace to love you and to serve you by following his example.

Almighty God, who manifested the power of St. Sharbel's intercession by numerous miracles and favors, grant us, through his intercession, this grace *(mention here)*. Amen.

191. Novena Prayer to Sts. Joachim & Ann
Grandparents of Jesus

Begin: July 17   *Feast Day: July 26*

Good parents of the Blessed Virgin Mary, grandparents of our Savior, Jesus Christ, when life seems barren, help us to trust in God's Mercy. When we are confused, help us to find the way to God. When we are lost in the desert, lead us to those whom God has called us to love. When our marriage seems lifeless, show us the eternal youth of the Lord. When we are selfish, teach us to cling only to that which lasts. When we are afraid, help us to trust in God. When we are ashamed, remind us that we are God's children. When we sin, lead us to do God's will.

You who know God's will for husband and wife help us to live chastely. You who know God's will for the family keep all families close to you. You who suffered without children intercede for all infertile couples. You who trusted in God's will, help us to trust God with complete surrender. You, who gave birth to the Blessed Mother, inspire couples to be co-creators with God. You who taught the Mother of God, teach us to nurture children and grandchildren in holy instruction. You whose hearts trusted in God hear our prayers for *(mention here)*. Pray with our Rosary Family that we may be holy families. Amen.

July: Month of the Precious Blood of Jesus Christ

192. Novena to St. John Vianney

Begin: July 27 *Feast Day: Aug 4*

O holy Curé of Ars, St. John Vianney, you loved God and faithfully served Him by serving His people as their priest. Now, as you are with our Father, you can continue to serve Him by presenting our petitions to Him directly. Remember the vulnerabilities, fears, and anxieties surrounding us, especially those plaguing priests. Please intercede for us in all our needs, especially *(mention here)*. O Priest of Ars, pray for us in a special way during this novena; we ask in the Name of Jesus our Lord. Amen.

193. Prayer of St. Ignatius of Loyola

Feast Day: July 31

Teach us, Good Lord, to serve You as You deserve; to give, and not to count the cost, to fight, and not to heed the wounds, to toil, and not to seek for rest, to labor, and not to ask for reward, except that of knowing that we are doing Your Holy Will. Amen.

August

Month of the Immaculate Heart

194. Immaculate Heart of Mary

O Immaculate Heart of Mary, refuge of sinners, I beg of you by the infinite merits of the Sacred Heart of Jesus and by the graces God has granted you since your Immaculate Conception, the grace of never going astray again. Mother, keep me, a sinner, constantly bathed in the light of your Immaculate Heart. Amen.

195. Act of Entrusting a Soul to the Immaculate Heart of Mary

Immaculate Heart of Mary, I entrust the salvation of *(Name) to you*, having great confidence that you will save them. Amen.

196. Our Lady, Queen of Angels

Feast Day: Aug 2

August Queen of Heaven! Sovereign Mistress of the Angels! You who received from God the power and mission to crush the head of Satan, we humbly ask you to send your Holy Legions, that, under your command and through your power, that they may chase the devils, fight them everywhere, rebuke their boldness, and repel them into the abyss.

Who is like unto God? Oh, good and tender Mother, you will always be our love and our hope. Oh, Mother, send the Holy Angels and Archangels to defend me and to keep the cruel enemy far from me. Holy Angels and Archangels defend us, protect us. Amen.

August: Month of the Immaculate Heart

197. Prayer of St. John Vianney

Feast Day: Aug 4

I love You, O my God and my only desire is to love You until the last breath of my life. I love You, O my Infinitely Lovable God, and I would rather die loving You than to live without loving You. I love You, Lor,d and the only grace I ask is to love You eternally. My God, if my tongue cannot say in every moment that I love You, I want my heart to repeat it to You as often as I draw breath. Amen.

198. Prayer to St. Philomena

Feast Day: Aug 11

Glorious virgin and martyr, St. Philomena, whose glory God has been pleased to manifest by shining miracles! We address ourselves to you with entire confidence. Obtain for us that, following your example, we may generously combat all that opposes the reign of Jesus Christ in our hearts, that He may ornament them with thy virtues, with that angelic purity of which you are so perfect a model; it order that, enkindled with a love for Jesus, we may walk constantly in the way He has pointed out to us, and partake one day of your eternal felicity. Amen.

199. Prayer to St. Maximilian Kolbe

Feast Day: Aug 14

St. Maximilian Kolbe, the faithful follower of St. Francis of Assisi, inflamed by the love of God, you dedicated your life to the practice of virtue and to the works of the apostolate. Look down with favor upon us who devoutly confide in your intercession. Having consecrated yourself to the Immaculate Virgin Mary, you inspired countless souls to holy life and various forms of the apostolate to do good to others and spread the kingdom of God. Obtain for us the grace by our lives and labors to draw many souls to Christ.

St. Maximilian Kolbe, you gave your life so that a family might not be deprived of a husband and father. By your heroic martyrdom of charity, teach us that the value of family life is also worth our sacrifices. Just as you found in Mary the channel of those graces that strengthened you to be faithful to her Son, help us also to rejoice in her, who was given to us as a mother by Jesus from the cross. Be with us, St. Maximilian, as we pray for the special needs of our family *(mention here)*. Amen.

200. Novena to Our Lady of the Assumption

Begin: Aug 7   *Feast Day: Aug 15*

Mary, my dear Mother and mighty Queen take and receive my poor heart with all its freedom and desires, all its love, and all the virtues and graces with which it may be adorned. All I am, all I might be, all I have and hold in the order of nature as well as of grace, I have received from God through your loving intercession, my Lady and Queen. Into your sovereign hands, I entrust all that it may be returned to its noble origin.

Mary, Queen of every heart, accept all that I am and bind me to you with the bonds of love, that I may be yours forever and may be able to say in all truth: "I belong to Jesus through Mary."

My Mother assumed into Heaven, I love you. Give me a greater love for Jesus and for you.

Mary assumed into Heaven and Queen of the Universe, ever-Virgin Mother of God, obtain peace and salvation for us through your prayers, for you have given birth to Christ the Lord, the Savior of all mankind.

Let us pray: Almighty, Ever-Living God, You raised to eternal glory the body and soul of the Immaculate Virgin Mary, Mother of Your Son. Grant that our minds may always be directed heavenward and that we may deserve to share in her glory. Amen.

August: Month of the Immaculate Heart
201. Litany of Our Lady of Knock

Feast Day: Aug 21

Our Lady of Knock, **Pray for us**
Refuge of Sinners,...
Queen Assumed into Heaven,...
Queen of the Rosary,...
Mother of Nazareth,...
Queen of Virgins,...
Help of Christians,...
Health of the Sick,...
Queen of Peace,...
Our Lady, Queen, and Mother,...
Our Lady, Mother of the Church,...
(mention here)
With the Angels and Saints, let us pray: Give praise to the Father Almighty, to His Son, Jesus Christ the Lord, and to the Spirit who lives in our hearts, both now and forever. Amen.

202. St. Pius X Intercession Prayer

Feast Day: Aug 21

Glorious Pope of the Eucharist, St. Pius X, you sought to restore all things in Christ. Obtain for me a true love of Jesus so that I may live only for him. Help me to acquire a lively fervor and a sincere will to strive for the sanctity of life so that I may avail myself of the riches of the Holy Eucharist in sacrifice and sacrament. By your love for Mary, Mother, and Queen of all, inflame my heart with tender devotion to her. Blessed model of the priesthood, obtain for us holy, dedicated priests, and increase vocations to the religious life. Dispel confusion, hatred, and anxiety, and incline our hearts to peace and concord so that all nations will place themselves under the sweet reign of Christ. Amen.

August: Month of the Immaculate Heart

203. Invocation of the Entire Heavenly Court

Feast Day: Aug 22

O Glorious Queen of Heaven and earth, Virgin Most Powerful, thou who hast the power to crush the head of the ancient serpent with thy heel, come and exercise this power flowing from the grace of thine Immaculate Conception. Shield us under the mantle of thy purity and love, draw us into the sweet abode of thy heart, and annihilate and render impotent the forces bent on destroying us.

Come Most Sovereign Mistress of the Holy Angels and Mistress of the Most Holy Rosary, thou who from the very beginning hast received from God the power and the mission to crush the head of Satan. We humbly beseech thee, send forth thy Holy Legions, that under thy command and by thy power they may pursue the evil spirits, encounter them on every side, resist their bold attack, and drive them far from us, harming no one on the way, binding them immobile to the foot of the Cross to be judged and sentenced by Jesus Christ, Thy Son, and to be disposed of by Him as He wills.

St. Joseph, Patron of the Universal Church, come to our aid in this grave battle against the forces of darkness, repel the attacks of the devil, and free your children, the Rosary Family, and all our loved ones, especially *(mention here)*, from the stronghold the enemy has on their souls.

St. Michael, summon the entire heavenly court to engage their forces in this fierce battle against the powers of hell. Come, O Prince of Heaven, with thy mighty sword and thrust into hell Satan and all the other evil spirits. O Guardian Angels, guide and protect us. Amen.

August: Month of the Immaculate Heart

204. Novena to Saint Monica

Begin: Aug 18   *Feast Day: Aug 26*

Dear Saint Monica, you were once the mournful mother of a prodigal son. Your faithfulness to prayer brought you and your son so close to God that you are now with him in eternity. By your intercession and God's grace, your son, St. Augustine, became a great and venerable Saint of the Church. Please take my request to God with the same fervor and persistence with which you prayed for your own son *(mention here)*.

With your needs, worries, and anxieties, you threw yourself on the mercy and providence of God. Through sorrow and pain, you constantly devoted yourself to God. Pray for me that I might join you in such a deep faith in God's goodness and mercy. Above all, dear Saint Monica, pray for me that I may, like your son, turn from my sin and become a great Saint for the glory of God. Amen.

205. Our Lady of Częstochowa

Feast Day: Aug 26

Holy Mother of Czestochowa, Thou art full of grace, goodness, and mercy. I consecrate to Thee all my thoughts, words, and actions, my soul and body. I beseech Thy blessings and especially prayers for my salvation. Today, I consecrate myself to Thee, Good Mother, totally, with body and soul, amid joy and sufferings to obtain for myself and others Thy blessings on this earth and eternal life in Heaven. Amen.

August: Month of the Immaculate Heart

206. Prayer of St. Augustine

Feast Day: Aug 28

Lord Jesus, our Savior, let us come to You.

Our hearts are cold; Lord, warm them with Your Selfless Love.

Our hearts are sinful; cleanse them with Your Precious Blood.

Our hearts are weak; strengthen them with Your Joyous Spirit.

Our hearts are empty; fill them with Your Divine Presence.

Lord Jesus, our hearts are Yours; possess them always and only for Yourself. Amen.

September

Month of the Seven Sorrows of Mary

207. Mother, Stand by Me in My Last Hours

by St Gabriel Francis Possenti

O Mother of Sorrows, by the anguish and love with which thou did stand at the Cross of Jesus, stand by me in my last agony. To thy maternal heart, I commend the last three hours of my life. Offer these hours to the Eternal Father in union with the agony of our dearest Lord, in atonement for my sins. Offer to the Eternal Father the Most Precious Blood of Jesus, mingled with your tears on Calvary, that I may obtain the grace of receiving Holy Communion with the most perfect love and contrition before my death and that I may breathe forth my soul in the adorable presence of Jesus. Dearest Mother, when the moment of my death has at last come, present me as your child to Jesus. Ask Him to forgive me for having offended Him, for I knew not what I did. Beg Him to receive me into His kingdom of glory to be united with Him forever. Amen

208. Prayer of St. Mother Teresa of Calcutta

Feast Day: Sept 5

Mary, I depend on you totally as a child on its mother, that in return, you may possess me, protect me, and transform me into Jesus. May the light of your faith dispel the darkness of my mind; may your profound humility take the place of my pride; may your contemplation replace the distractions of my wandering imagination; and may your virtues take the place of my sins. Lead me deeper into the mystery of the Cross so that you may share your experience of Jesus' thirst with me. Amen.

September: Month of the Seven Sorrows of Mary

209. Nativity of the Blessed Virgin Mary Prayer

Feast Day: Sept 8

Impart to Your servants, we pray, O Lord, the gift of heavenly grace, that the Feast of the Nativity of the Blessed Virgin may bring deeper peace to those for whom the birth of her Son was the dawning of salvation. Through our Lord Jesus Christ, Your Son, who lives and reigns with You in the unity of the Holy Spirit, God, forever and ever. Amen.

210. Novena Prayer for the Intercession of St. Pio of Pietrelcina

Begin: Sept. 14 *Feast Day: Sept 22*

Dear God, You generously blessed Your servant, St. Pio of Pietrelcina, with the gifts of the Spirit. You marked his body with the five wounds of Christ Crucified as a powerful witness to the saving Passion and Death of Your Son. Endowed with the gift of discernment, St. Pio labored endlessly in the confessional for the salvation of souls. With reverence and intense devotion in the celebration of Mass, he invited countless men and women to a greater union with Jesus Christ in the Sacrament of the Holy Eucharist. Through the intercession of St. Padre Pio, I confidently beseech You to grant me the grace of *(mention here)*. Amen.

September: Month of the Seven Sorrows of Mary

211. Our Lady of Sorrows

Feast Day: Sept 15

Mother of Sorrows, your heart suffered so much. I beg you by the merits of tears you shed to obtain for me, and all sinners, the grace of complete sincerity and repentance. Amen.

Our Lady of Sorrows, reveal to me that evil that is attacking me (or spouse, or children). Amen.

212. The Seven Sorrows Rosary

This rosary is a little different. It is seven (7) decades- each decade has one (1) Our Father and seven (7) Hail Marys. There are different prayers listed below.

Introductory Prayer: My God, I offer You this Rosary for Your glory so I can honor your Holy Mother, the Blessed Virgin so that I can share and meditate upon her suffering. I humbly beg you to give me true repentance for all my sins. Give me wisdom and humility so that I may receive all the indulgences contained in this prayer. Amen.

Act of Contrition: O my God, I am heartily sorry for having offended You, and I detest all my sins because I dread the loss of Heaven and the pains of hell; but most of all because I have offended You, my God, You Who are all good and deserving of all my love. I firmly resolve, with the help of Your grace, to confess my sins, to do penance, and to avoid the near occasion of sin. Amen.

3 Hail Marys in honor of Mary's tears.

Pray: Most Merciful Mother, remind us always about the Sorrows of your Son, Jesus. Amen.

September: Month of the Seven Sorrows of Mary

The First Sword of Sorrow:
The Prophecy of Simeon
(Luke 2:22-35)
1-Our Father, 7-Hail Mary's

End Prayer: Most Merciful Mother, remind us always about the Sorrows of your Son, Jesus.

The Second Sword of Sorrow:
The Flight into Egypt
(Matthew 2:13-15)
1-Our Father, 7-Hail Mary's

End Prayer: Most Merciful Mother, remind us always about the Sorrows of your Son, Jesus.

The Third Sword of Sorrow:
The Loss of Jesus in the Temple
(Luke 2:41-52)
1-Our Father, 7-Hail Mary's

End Prayer: Most Merciful Mother, remind us always about the Sorrows of your Son, Jesus.

The Fourth Sword of Sorrow:
Mary Meets Jesus on the Way to Calvary
(Luke 23:27-31)
1-Our Father, 7-Hail Mary's

End Prayer: Most Merciful Mother, remind us always about the Sorrows of your Son, Jesus.

The Fifth Sword of Sorrow:
Mary Stands at the Foot of the Cross
(John 19:25-27)
1-Our Father, 7-Hail Mary's

End Prayer: Most Merciful Mother, remind us always about the Sorrows of your Son, Jesus.

September: Month of the Seven Sorrows of Mary

The Sixth Sword of Sorrow:
Mary Receives the Dead Body of Jesus
(John 19:38-40)
1-Our Father, 7-Hail Mary's

End Prayer: Most Merciful Mother, remind us always about the Sorrows of your Son, Jesus.

The Seventh Sword of Sorrow:
The Body of Jesus is Placed in the Tomb
(John 19:41-42)
1-Our Father, 7-Hail Mary's

End Prayer: Most Merciful Mother, remind us always about the Sorrows of your Son, Jesus.

Concluding Prayer: Queen of Martyrs, your heart suffered so much. I beg you, by the merits of the tears you shed in these terrible and sorrowful times, to obtain for me and all the sinners of the world the grace of complete sincerity and repentance. Amen.

Pray: Mary, who was conceived without sin and who suffered for us, pray for us. *(3xs)*

September: Month of the Seven Sorrows of Mary
213. Prayer to Mary, Undoer of Knots

Feast Day: Sept 28

Holy Mary, Undoer of Knots, and our Mother, to you who untie with a motherly heart the knots of our lives, pray for us, your children:

who have struggling families, **undo our knot**

who are beset by financial struggles,...

who are seeking employment,...

who are suffering from mental and physical illness,...

who are homeless or destitute,...

who are tied up in the evil one's lies and confusion,...

who are burdened with loneliness, fears, anxieties, or worries,...

who are living with addictions,...

who have fallen away from God and the Holy Catholic Church,...

who have been abused by those we trusted,...

who are enduring religious or ethnic persecution,...

who are overwhelmed by shame, depression, or despair,...

who are traumatized by events in our lives,...

who are struggling to let go of grudges and to extend forgiveness,...

who do not seek repentance or holiness,...

who are tied to our sin more than God,...

who hurt those we love with our words or actions,...

who judge quickly and speak sharply,...

who feel the burden of guilt or regret,...

who are suffering,...

O Mother! You know the difficulties, sorrow, and pain we have in our lives. O Mary, I place the ribbon of my life and these knots into your loving hands, hands which can undo even the most difficult knot. Most holy Mother, come to my aid and intercede for me before God with your prayers. I cast these knots into your hands *(mention here)* and beg you to undo them, in the name of your son, Jesus Christ, and for the glory of God, once and for all. Our Lady, Undoer of Knots, pray for us!

214. Consecration Prayer to St. Michael

Feast Day: Sept 29

O Saint Michael the Archangel, I join you in your adorations and thanksgiving towards God and in your praises towards the Most Holy Virgin; please make up for my insufficiency. Saint Michael, I consecrate myself to you; protect me today and during my whole life and at the moment of my death. Saint Michael the Archangel, defend us in the battle so that we may not perish on the dreadful day of judgment. Saint Michael, pray for us, repel Satan and all evil spirits into hell, and save the world. Amen.

215. The Chaplet of St. Michael the Archangel

O Glorious Prince St. Michael, chief and commander of the heavenly hosts, guardian of souls, vanquisher of rebel spirits, servant in the house of the Divine King, and our admirable conductor, thou who dost shine with excellence and superhuman virtue, vouchsafe to deliver us from all evil, who turn to thee with confidence and enable us by thy gracious protection to serve God more and more faithfully every day.

Pray for us, O glorious St. Michael, Prince of the Church of Jesus Christ. That we may be made worthy of His promises.

Almighty and Everlasting God, Who by a prodigy of goodness and a merciful desire for the salvation of all men, hast appointed the most glorious Archangel, St. Michael, Prince of Thy Church, make us worthy, we beseech Thee, to be delivered from all our enemies that none of them may harass us at the hour of death, but that we may be conducted by him into the august presence of Thy Divine Majesty. This we beg through the merits of Jesus Christ, our Lord. Amen.

September: Month of the Seven Sorrows of Mary

216. Act of Entrustment to St. Michael

The most glorious prince of the Angelic Hosts, valiant warrior of the Most High, zealous lover of God's glory, terror of rebellious angels, love and delight of righteous Angels Saint Michael the Archangel, desiring to be among your devotees, I offer myself to You. I put myself, my work, my family, my friends, and what belongs to me under your vigilant protection. Being a poor sinner, my sacrifice is poor, but you will not despise my heart. Remember that from now on, I will be under Your special protection, so please assist me throughout my life. Obtain for me the forgiveness of my many and grave sins, the grace to cherish with all my heart my God, dear Saviour Jesus Christ, the sweetest Mother Mary and all people, my brothers, beloved by God the Father and redeemed by God's Son. Plead for all the help I need to receive the crown of heavenly glory. Always defend me from the enemies of my soul, especially in the last moment of my life. Come to my help, oh glorious Archangel, assist me in the struggle and reject away from me, in the abysses of Hell, that arrogant and proud angel whom you defeated and humiliated during the celestial battle. Lead me to the Throne of God the Most High, that I may praise with You, Saint Michael the Archangel, and with all the Angels, honor, glory, and thanksgiving to Him who lives and reigns forever and ever. Amen!

September: Month of the Seven Sorrows of Mary

217. Mary, Queen of the Angels

O Mary, Queen of the Angels, send me St Michael, your Archangel, to defend and secure me all my life and assist me in my last moment. O Immaculate Mary, our sweet Mediatrix, the Queen of Heaven and Earth, we beseech you very humbly, dain to intercede for us again. Ask God to send St. Michael and his Angels to clear all the obstacles that hinder the reign of the Sacred Heart in souls, in families, and in the whole of Chrisitan Society. Amen.

218. St. Michael Consecration Prayer

St. Michael the Archangel, I consecrate to you my soul and body. I choose you as my patron and protector. Be my strength and the guardian in my life. Assist me by your powerful intercession so that I may imitate your courage and loyalty to God, that trusting in your kind help and protection, I may be victorious over the enemies of my soul and be united with God in heaven forever and ever. Amen.

219. Prayer to Sts. Michael, Gabriel & Raphael

Feast Day: Sept 29

Heavenly Father, thank You for giving us Archangels to assist us during our pilgrimage on earth. St. Michael, our protector, come to my aid, fight for me and all my loved ones, and protect us from danger.

St. Gabriel, messenger of the Good News, help me clearly hear your voice and to teach me to hear truth, which is Christ.

St. Raphael, wonderful healer, take my need for healing and that of everyone I know, lift it up to Our Heavenly King's Throne of Grace and deliver us back to the gift of recovery. Help us, O Lord, to realize more fully the reality of Archangels and their desire to serve us. Holy Angels, pray for us. Amen.

September: Month of the Seven Sorrows of Mary

220. Miraculous Invocation to St. Therese of Lisieux

Begin: Sept. 22 *Feast Day: Oct 1*

Glorious St. Therese, whom Almighty God has raised up to aid and inspire the human family, I implore your Miraculous Intercession for our Rosary Family. You are so powerful in obtaining every need of body and spirit from the Heart of God. Holy Mother Church proclaims you 'Prodigy of Miracles, the Greatest Saint of Modern Times." Now I fervently beseech you to answer my petition *(mention here)* and to carry out your promises of spending Heaven doing good on earth, of letting fall from Heaven a "Shower of Roses."

Little Flower, give me your childlike faith to see the Face of God in the people and experiences of my life and to love God with complete confidence. St. Therese, my Carmelite Sister, I will fulfill your plea to be made known everywhere and continue to lead others to Jesus through you. Amen.

October

Month of the Holy Rosary

221. Consecration to the Holy Guardian Angel

Feast Day: Oct 2

Holy Guardian Angel, You continually behold the face of our Father in heaven. God entrusted me to you from the very beginning of my life. I thank you with all my heart for your loving care. I commit myself to you and promise you my love and fidelity.

I beg you, protect me against my own weakness and against the attacks of the wicked spirits; enlighten my mind and my heart so that I may always know and accomplish the Holy Will of God; and lead me to union with God the Father, the Son, and the Holy Spirit (+). Amen.

222. Invocations of the Holy Guardian Angels

Holy Angel, my counselor, inspire me.
Holy Angel, my defender, protect me.
Holy Angel, my faithful friend, intercede for me.
Holy Angel, my consoler, fortify me.
Holy Angel, my brother, defend me.
Holy Angel, my teacher, instruct me.
Holy Angel, witness of all my actions, purify me.
Holy Angel, my helper, support me.
Holy Angel, my intercessor, speak for me.
Holy Angel, my guide, direct me.
Holy Angel, my light, enlighten me.
Holy Angel, whom God has assigned to lead me, govern me.

October: Month of the Holy Rosary

223. Peace Prayer of St. Francis of Assisi

Feast Day: Oct 4

Lord, make me an instrument of your peace: where there is hatred, let me sow love; where there is injury, pardon; where there is doubt, faith; where there is despair, hope; where there is darkness, light; where there is sadness, joy.

O Divine Master, grant that I may not so much seek to be consoled as to console, to be understood as to understand, to be loved as to love. For it is in giving that we receive, it is in pardoning that we are pardoned, and it is in dying that we are born to eternal life. Amen.

224. Prayer for the Canonization of Blessed Carlo Acutis

Feast Day: Oct 12

Oh God, Our Father, thank You for giving us Carlo, an example for the young people and a message of love for everyone. You made him fall in love with Your Son, Jesus, making the Eucharist his "Highway to Heaven." You gave him Mary as beloved Mother, and, with the Rosary, you made him sing the praises of her tenderness. Accept his prayer for us.

Above all, gaze upon the poor, whom he loved and helped. Through his intercession, may I receive the grace of *(mention here)* and fulfill our joy by placing Carlo among the Saints of your Church so that his smile may shine again for us in the glory of Your name. Amen.

October: Month of the Holy Rosary

225. Novena for All Saints Day

Begin: Oct. 23rd   *Feast Day: Nov. 1*

Protect Thy people, O Lord: And, as we confide in the patronage of Thy Apostles, Peter and Paul, and the other Apostles, so preserve and defend us continually. May all Thy Saints, we beseech Thee, O Lord, everywhere assist us; that while we celebrate their merits, we may find their patronage. Grant us Thy peace in our time, and drive away all wickedness from Thy Church. Direct our ways, our actions and desires, and those of all Thy servants, in the prosperity of Thy saving conduct: Grant to our benefactors eternal blessings, and to the faithful departed, everlasting rest.

O Blessed Saints of Paradise, the glorious Citizens of Heaven, as I render most humble thanks to God for all the good He has done you; I beseech you to remember me in your prayers and obtain for me the entire remission of my sins, the amendment of my life, and the imitation of your good spirit, and the holy graces, that I may be perfectly reconciled to my Savior, and always be pleasing to Him, especially I recommend to you the hour of my death, that by your holy intercession my soul may depart this world in the grace of God, and immediately come to Life Everlasting. Amen.

November

Month of the Holy Souls in Purgatory

226. O Gentlest Heart of Jesus

Feast Day: Nov. 2

O most gentle Heart of Jesus, ever present in the Blessed Sacrament, ever consumed with burning love for the poor captive souls in Purgatory, have mercy on the souls of Thy departed servants *(Name)*. Be not severe in Thy judgments, but let some drops of Thy Precious Blood fall upon the devouring flames. And do Thou, O merciful Savior, send Thy holy Angels to conduct them to a place of refreshment, light, and peace. Amen.

227. Prayer to the Sacred Heart for those in Purgatory

Most Sacred Heart of Jesus, remembering the promise of the Resurrection, I humbly and sincerely offer these prayers and Masses for *(mention here)* and all the departed. With joy, I thank You for what we shared in this earthly life. With hope, I pray this offering will help them on their journey to the fullness of life and happiness with You in Heaven. Purify them from all that is not holy so they may dwell in the mystery of Your Perfect Love forever. With blessed anticipation, I look forward to the coming age when, with Your grace, I shall be united with them again in Paradise. Amen.

November: Month of the Holy Souls in Purgatory

228. Prayer of Deliverance for the Poor Souls

My Jesus, by the Sorrows Thou didst suffer in Thine agony in the Garden, in Thy Scourging and Crowning with thorns, on the way to Calvary, in Thy Crucifixion and Death, have mercy on the souls in purgatory, and especially on those that are most forsaken; do Thou deliver them from the terrible torments they endure; call them and admit them to Thy most sweet embrace in paradise.

O Most Gentle Heart of Jesus, ever present in the Most Blessed Sacrament of the Altar. Ever consumed with burning love for the poor Catholic souls in Purgatory, have mercy on the souls of Thy departed servants. Be not severe in Thy judgment, but let dome drop of Thy Precious Blood fall upon the devouring flames, and do Thou O Merciful Savior, send your Holy Angels to conduct them to a place of refreshment, life, and peace. Amen.

229. Prayer of St. Gertrude the Great

to release 1,000 souls

Eternal Father, I offer You the Most Precious Blood of Thy Divine Son, Jesus, in union with the Masses said throughout the world today, for all the Holy Souls in purgatory, for sinners everywhere, for sinners in the universal Church, those in my own home and within my family. Amen

230. Prayer of Blessed Miguel Pro.

Feast Day: Nov. 23

I believe, O Lord, but strengthen my faith. Heart of Jesus, I love Thee, but increase my love. Heart of Jesus, I trust in Thee but give greater vigor to my confidence. Heart of Jesus, I give my heart to Thee, but so enclose it in Thee that it may never be separated from Thee. Heart of Jesus, I am all Thine, but take care of my promise so that I may be able to put it into practice even unto the complete sacrifice of my life. Amen.

November: Month of the Holy Souls in Purgatory

231. Prayer to St. Joseph for a Soul in Purgatory

Great St. Joseph, who so tenderly loved Jesus and felt so keenly the loss of His Presence during the time that you were in Limbo, I earnestly recommend to you our Rosary Family, the souls of their loved ones, and especially the souls of *(mention name)*, who may at this moment be suffering in Purgatory. Be their consoler in that place of suffering and expiation! Deign to apply to them the pious suffrages of the faithful, particularly my own; be their intercessor with Jesus and Mary and obtain by your prayers that, delivered from the bonds that hold them in captivity, they may fly to the bosom of God, there to be eternally in the enjoyment of those delights with which the elect are blessed. Amen.

232. An Act of Mercy for Souls Suffering in Purgatory

Immaculate Mary, Mother of Mercy, who saw the Sacred Body of Your Beloved Son raised on the Cross, looked at the soil soaked with His Blood and were present at His cruel Death, we offer you, most Holy Mother, the souls suffering in purgatory, and we beg you to be so kind as to look upon them with your merciful eyes and ask for their release from their torments. In order to receive your forgiveness, O Immaculate Mother, we sincerely and heartily forgive all those who have insulted us, and through your intercession, we beg Jesus to grant them every goodness, grace, and blessing in exchange for the wrong they did to us or wished upon us. Through your hands, O Holy Virgin, we offer to the Lord this act of love, asking His mercy for the souls that are being purged. Amen.

November: Month of the Holy Souls in Purgatory
233. Prayers for the Deceased for Every Day of the Week

Sunday: O Lord God Omnipotent, I ask You by the Precious Blood, which Your Divine Son, Jesus, shed in the Garden, deliver the souls in purgatory, and especially that one which is the most forsaken of all, and bring it into Your glory, where it may praise and bless You forever. Amen.

Monday: O Lord God Omnipotent, I ask You by the Precious Blood which Your Divine Son, Jesus, shed in cruel scourging, deliver the souls in purgatory, and among them all, especially that soul which is nearest to its entrance into Your glory, that it may soon praise You and bless You forever. Amen.

Tuesday: O Lord God Omnipotent, I ask You by the Precious Blood of Your Divine Son, Jesus, that was shed in His bitter crowning with thorns, deliver the souls in purgatory, and among them all, particularly that soul which is in the greatest need of our prayers, in order that it may not long be delayed in praising You in Your glory and blessing You forever. Amen.

Wednesday: O Lord God Omnipotent, I ask You by the Precious Blood of Your Divine Son, Jesus, that was shed in the streets of Jerusalem while He carried on His sacred shoulders the heavy burden of the Cross, deliver the souls in purgatory and especially that one which is richest in merits in Your sight, so that, having soon attained the high place in glory to which it is destined, it may praise You triumphantly and bless You forever. Amen.

November: Month of the Holy Souls in Purgatory

Thursday: O Lord God Omnipotent, I ask You by the Precious Body and Blood of Your Divine Son, Jesus, which He Himself on the night before His Passion gave as food and drink to His beloved Apostles and bequeathed to His Holy Church the perpetual Sacrifice and life-giving nourishment of His faithful people, deliver the souls in purgatory, but most of all, that soul which was most devoted to this mystery of infinite love, in order that it may praise You together with Your divine Son and the Holy Spirit in Your glory forever. Amen.

Friday: O Lord God Omnipotent, I ask You by the Precious Blood, which Jesus, Your Divine Son, shed this day upon the tree of the Cross, especially from His Sacred Hands and Feet, deliver the souls in purgatory, and particularly that soul for whom I am most bound to pray, in order that I may not be the cause which hinders You from admitting it quickly to the possession of Your glory where it may praise and bless You forever more. Amen.

Saturday: O Lord God Omnipotent, I ask You by the Precious Blood, which gushed forth from the Sacred Side of Your Divine Son, Jesus, in the presence and to the great sorrow of His Most Holy Mother, deliver the souls in purgatory and among them all especially that soul which has been most devout to Our Lady, that it may come quickly into Your glory, there to praise You in her and her in You through all the ages. Amen.

November: Month of the Holy Souls in Purgatory

234. Prayer to St. Cecilia

Feast Day: Nov. 22

O glorious St. Cecilia, virgin and martyr, you won the martyr's crown without renouncing your love for Jesus, the delight of your soul. We ask that you help us to be faithful in our love for Jesus, that, in the Communion of the Saints, we may praise Him twice in our song of rejoicing for the Blood that He shed, which gave us the grace to accomplish His will on earth. Amen.

235. An Act of Thanksgiving

What shall I render to the Lord for all the favors and graces He has bestowed upon me? What great blessings, both known and unknown, have I not received, and I have replied only with ingratitude to all this. But having Thee, O Lord Jesus Christ, in my heart, I can, at this very moment, pay my whole debt of gratitude to almighty God. For this purpose, I unite myself to that infinite act of thanksgiving rising continually from Thy Sacred Heart. Thou knowest well all the gifts I have received from Thy Divine Goodness ever since I was placed in the world and born again to the Life of Grace. Do Thou, O Lord, render for me due thanks to the most Holy Trinity, since to unite with Thine Own giving of thanks do I desire to make my thanksgiving consists. Amen.

November: Month of the Holy Souls in Purgatory

236. Act of Consecration to Our Lady of the Miraculous Medal

Apparition: Nov. 27, 1830

O Virgin Mother of God, Mary Immaculate, we dedicate and consecrate ourselves to you under the title of Our Lady of the Miraculous Medal. May this Medal be for each one of us, a sure sign of your affection for us and a constant reminder of our duties towards you. Ever while wearing it, may we be blessed by your loving protection and preserved in the grace of your Son. O most powerful Virgin, Mother of our Savior, keep us close to you every moment of our lives. Obtain for us, your children, the grace of a happy death so that, in union with you, we may enjoy the bliss of heaven forever. Amen

Mary, conceived without sin, pray for us who have recourse to you. *(3 xs)*

November: Month of the Holy Souls in Purgatory

237. Prayer to Our Lady of Kibeho

Feast Day: Nov. 28

Blessed Virgin Mary, Mother of the Word, Mother of all those who believe in Him and welcome Him into their lives, we have come here before you to contemplate you. We believe that you are among us, as a mother with her children, even if we can not see you with our eyes. You are a sure path which leads us to Jesus the Savior.

We bless you for all the good things that you continue to give us, especially because you consented to appear in a miraculous way at Kibeho at the time when our world needed you so much.

Give us always the light and the strength we need to eagerly welcome your call to convert ourselves, to repent, and to live according to the Gospel of your Son. Teach us to pray without hypocrisy and to love one another as He loved us so that, as you have asked us, we might always be like beautiful flowers with beautiful perfume spreading everywhere.

O Holy Mary, Our Lady of Sorrows, teaches us to understand the value of the Cross in our lives. By offering our sufferings to his help us to complete in our own flesh what is missing in the sufferings of Christ in favor of his Mystical Body, which is the Church. And when our pilgrimage here on earth has ended, we will live forever with you in the Kingdom of Heaven. Amen.

November: Month of the Holy Souls in Purgatory

238. Novena to the Immaculate Conception

Begin: Nov 29 *Feast Day: Dec 8*

Immaculate Virgin Mary, you were pleasing in the sight of God from the first moment of your conception in the womb of your mother, St. Anne. You were chosen to be the Mother of Jesus Christ, the Son of God. I believe the teaching of Holy Mother the Church that in the first instant of your conception, by the singular grace and privilege of Almighty God, in virtue of the merits of Jesus Christ, Savior of the human race and beloved Son, you were preserved from all stain of original sin. I thank God for this wonderful privilege and grace He bestowed upon you as I honor your Immaculate Conception. Look graciously upon me as I implore this special favor *(mention here)*.

Virgin Immaculate, Mother of God and my Mother, from your throne in Heaven, turn your eyes of pity upon me. Filled with confidence in your goodness and power, I beg you to help me in this journey of life, which is so full of dangers for my soul. I entrust myself entirely to you that I may never be the slave of the devil through sin but may always live a humble and pure life. I consecrate myself to you forever, for my only desire is to love your Divine Son Jesus. Mary, since none of your devout servants has perished, may I too be saved. Amen.

November: Month of the Holy Souls in Purgatory

239. Christ the King Prayer

Feast Day: Sunday before Advent

Lord Jesus Christ, our Savior and our King renew my allegiance to Your Kingship.

I pray for the grace to place You above the powers of this world in all things.

I pray for the grace to obey You before any civic authority.

I pray for the grace to fervently bring about Your Kingdom in my family and community.

I pray that You will reign in my mind.
I pray that You will reign in my heart.
I pray that You will reign in my will.
I pray that You will reign in my body.
I pray that You will reign throughout all the world.
I pray that You will reign in every area of my life.
O Prince of Peace, may Your reign be complete in my life and in the life of the world. As I reflect on Your second, glorious coming and the judgment of all mankind, I beg You to show me mercy and give me the grace to become a great Saint. I pray that not only will I spend eternity with You but that You may use me, a sinner, to bring others into Your Kingdom for Your glory. Amen

December

Month of the Immaculate Conception

240. St. Andrew Christmas Novena

Begin: Nov 30   *Feast Day: Dec 25*

Hail and blessed be the hour and the moment in which the Son of God was born of the most pure Virgin Mary, at midnight in Bethlehem, in the piercing cold. In that hour, vouchsafe, I beseech Thee, O my God, to hear my prayer and grant my desires, through the merits of Our Saviour Jesus Christ, and of His Blessed Mother. Amen. *(15x)*

It is piously believed that whoever recites the above prayer fifteen times a day from the Feast of St. Andrew (Nov. 30th) until Christmas will obtain what is asked.

241. Prayer of the Immaculate Conception

Solemnity: Dec 8

O God, Who by the Immaculate Conception of the Blessed Virgin Mary, didst prepare a worthy dwelling place for Thy Son, we beseech Thee that, as by the foreseen death of this, Thy Son, Thou didst preserve her from all stain, so tooTthou wouldst permit us, purified through her intercession, to come unto Thee. Through the same Lord Jesus Christ, Thy Son, who livest and reignest with Thee in the unity of the Holy Spirit, God, world without end. Amen.

242. Prayer to Venerable Fulton Sheen

Feast Day: Dec 9

Eternal Father, You alone grant us every blessing in Heaven and on earth through the redemptive mission of Your Divine Son, Jesus Christ, and by the working of the Holy Spirit. If it is according to Your Will, glorify Your servant, Archbishop Fulton J. Sheen, by granting the favor I now request through his prayerful intercession *(mention here)*. I make this prayer confidently through Jesus Christ, Our Lord. Amen.

December: Month of the Immaculate Conception

243. Prayer to the Virgin of Guadalupe
By St. John Paul II

Feast Day: Dec 12

O Virgin of Guadalupe, Mother of the Americas, grant to our homes the grace of loving and respecting life in its beginnings, with the same love with which you conceived in your womb the life of the Son of God. Blessed Virgin Mary, Mother of Fair Love, protect our families so that they may always be united and bless the upbringing of our children.

Our Hope look upon us with pity, teach us to go continually to Jesus, and if we fall, help us to rise again and return to Him through the confession of our faults and our sins in the Sacrament of Penance, which gives peace to the soul.

We beg you to grant us a great love of all the Holy Sacraments, which are, as it were, the signs that your Son left us on earth. Thus, Most Holy Mother, with the peace of God in our consciences, with our hearts free from evil and hatred, we will be able to bring to all others true joy and true peace, which come to us from your Son, our Lord Jesus Christ, who with the Father and the Holy Spirit, lives and reigns forever and ever. Amen.

244. Prayer to St. Lucy

Feast Day: Dec 13

O St Lucy, preserve the light of my eyes so that I may see the beauties of creation, the glow of the sun, the color of the flowers, and the smile of children. Preserve also the eyes of my soul, the faith, through which I can know my God, understand His teachings, recognize His love for me, and never miss the road that leads me to where you, St Lucy, can be found in the company of the Angels and Saints. St Lucy, protect my eyes and preserve my faith! St. Lucy, pray for us! Amen.

245. Traditional Prayer to Jesus in the Manger

O Divine Redeemer Jesus Christ, prostrate before Your crib; I believe You are the God of Infinite Majesty, even though I do not see You here as but a helpless babe. I humbly adore and thank You for having so humbled Yourself for my salvation as to will to be born in a stable. I thank You for all You wished to suffer for me in Bethlehem: for the poverty and humility, for the nakedness, tears, cold, and suffering. Would that I could show You the tenderness which Your Virgin Mother had towards You and love You as she did. Would that I could praise You with the joy of the Angels, that I could kneel before You with the faith of St. Joseph or the simplicity of the shepherds.

Uniting myself with these first adorers at the crib, I offer to You the homage of my heart, and I beg that You would be born spiritually in my soul. Make me reflect to some degree on the virtues of Your Admirable Nativity. Fill me with that spirit of renunciation, of poverty, of humility, which prompted You to assume the weakness of our nature and to be born amid destitution and suffering. Grant that from this day forward, I may in all things seek Your greater glory and may enjoy that peace promised to men of goodwill. Amen.

Artist: Amber Knorr

246. Novena to the Infant Jesus of Prague

O Jesus, Who said, "Ask and you shall receive, seek and you shall find, knock and it shall be opened to you," through the intercession of Mary, Your Most Holy Mother, I knock, I seek, I ask that my prayer be answered *(mention here)*.

O Jesus, Who said, "All that you ask of the Father in My Name He will grant you," through the intercession of Mary, Your Most Holy Mother, I humbly and urgently ask Your Father in Your Name that my prayer be granted *(mention here)*.

O Jesus, Who said, "Heaven and earth shall pass away, but My word shall not pass away," through the intercession of Mary, Your Most Holy Mother, I feel confident that my prayer will be granted *(mention here)*. Amen.

247. O Holy Infant, Jesus of Good Health

O Holy Infant Jesus of Good Health, I believe in the Infinite Goodness of Your Heart. Mercifully help me in my present necessity.

O Holy Infant Jesus of Good Health, I hope in the Boundless Mercy You show to those who humbly look up to You for help. Mercifully hear my petition and grant me the favor of Your kind help.

O Holy Infant Jesus of Good Health, I love you with all my heart. I entrust and consecrate myself to Your Most Loving Heart. Do hear my plea. I implore You and mercifully extend Your Helping Hand to me. Amen.

December: Month of the Immaculate Conception

248. Novena to St. Elizabeth Ann Seton

Begin: Dec 26   *Feast Day: Jan 4*

O Father, the first rule of our dear Savior's life was to do Your will. Let His will of the present moment be the first rule of our daily life and work, with no other desire but for its most full and complete accomplishment. Help us to follow it faithfully so that doing what You wish we will be pleasing to You.

We ask in particular for *(mention here)* through the intercession of St Elizabeth Ann Seton in this novena.

Lord Jesus, who was born for us in a stable, lived for us a life of pain and sorrow, and died for us upon a Cross; say for us in the hour of death, Father, forgive, and to Thy Mother, Behold thy child. Say to us: This day you shall be with Me in paradise.

Dear Savior, leave us not, forsake us not. We thirst for You, Fountain of Living Water. Our days pass quickly along, and soon, all will be consummated for us. Into Your hands, we commend our spirits, now and forever, Amen.

St Elizabeth Ann Seton, pray for us!

249. Feast of the Holy Innocents

O God, whom the Holy Innocents confessed and proclaimed on this day, not by speaking but by dying, grant, we pray, that the faith in You which we confess with our lips may also speak through our manner of life. Through our Lord Jesus Christ, Your Son, who lives and reigns with You in the unity of the Holy Spirit, God, forever and ever. Amen.

December: Month of the Immaculate Conception

250. Prayer to the Holy Family

O Jesus, Son of God and Son of Mary, bless our family. Graciously inspire in us the unity, peace, and mutual love that You found in Your own family in the little town of Nazareth.

O Mary, Mother of Jesus and Our Mother nourish our family with your faith and your love. Keep us close to your Son, Jesus, in all our sorrows and joys.

O Good St. Joseph, Foster-father to Jesus, spouse of Mary, guardian of your family, keep our family safe from harm. Help us in all times of discouragement or anxiety.

Holy Family of Nazareth, make our family one with you. Help us to be instruments of peace. Grant that love, strengthened by grace, may prove mightier than all the weaknesses and trials through which our families sometimes pass. May we always have God at the center of our hearts and homes until we are all one family, happy and at peace in our true home with you in Heaven. Amen.

December: Month of the Immaculate Conception
251. Intercession of Servant of God, Fr. John A. Hardon

Feast Day: Dec 30

O, God, You gave Your servant, Fr. John Anthony Hardon, while on earth, a deep devotion to You in the Holy Eucharist, a profound love of Our Lady of the Rosary, the revelation of a great theologian, and the heart of a humble priest of the Society of Jesus. Ever devoted to Our Lady, he sought to follow her instructions she gave the servants in Cana, "Do whatever He tells you." *(Jn 2:5)*. May his many teachings of the Catholic Church, his heroic example of life, and his devotion to Our Lady, inspire each of us to draw us closer to You in the Eucharist.

We humbly ask that You glorify Your Servant of God, Fr. John Anthony Hardon, on earth with the magnitude of Saints according to the design of Your Holy Will. Through his intercession, grant the favor I now present *(mention here)*. We ask this through Christ our Lord, in union with Our Lady of the Rosary. Amen.

Litanies

15 Promises of the Rosary

Promises 11-15

11. By the recitation of the Rosary, you shall obtain all that you ask of me.
12. Those who propagate the Holy Rosary shall be aided by me in their necessities.
13. I have obtained from my Divine Son that all the advocates of the Rosary shall have for intercessors the entire celestial court during their life and at the hour of their death.
14. All who recite the Rosary are my beloved children and the brothers and sisters of my only Son, Jesus Christ.
15. Devotion for my Rosary is a great sign of predestination.

252. Litany of Resignation to the Holy Will of God

Lord, have mercy on us. Christ, have mercy on us.
Lord, have mercy on us. Jesus, hear us, Jesus, graciously hear us.

God the Father, Who has created me, ***Hallowed be Your will.***
God the Son, Who has redeemed me, ***Not my will but Yours be done.***
God the Holy Ghost, Who has offered sanctification, ***Blessed be the Most Sweet Will of God.***
You know and foresee all things, ***Have mercy on us.***
You Who govern and rule all things,...
You Who rule according to inscrutable designs effects all things in a wonderful manner,...
Thou Who permit evil in order then to derive good for the salvation of the elect,...

In all things and in all possible events, ***Your Holy Will be done, my God.***
In all circumstances and disgraces,...
In my state and employment,...
In my affairs and occupations,...
In all my actions,...
In my health and strength,...
In my body and soul,...
In my life and death,...
In all men and angels,...
In all creatures,...
In all parts of the earth, and at all times,...
In myself and in those who belong to me,...
For all eternity,...
Although weak nature complains,...
Because You are my Creator,...
Because You are the Supreme Lord of all things,...
Although it costs much to self-love and sensuality,...

Solely and only through love for Thee and Thy good pleasure, **Your Holy Will be done, my God.**

Because You are infinite perfection,...

Therefore I say with all the Saints in Heaven, and with the Blessed Virgin Mary,...

With Jesus in the Garden of Olives,...

May the just, most amiable Will of God be done in all things.
May it be praised and magnified forever! Amen.

253. Litany of the Sacred Heart of Jesus

Lord, have mercy. Christ, have mercy.
Lord, have mercy. Christ, hear us. Christ, graciously hear us.

God, the Father of Heaven, **have mercy on us.**
God, the Son, Redeemer of the world, ...
God, the Holy Spirit,...
Holy Trinity, One God,...
Heart of Jesus, Son of the eternal Father,
Heart of Jesus, formed by the Holy Spirit in the womb of the Virgin Mother,...
Heart of Jesus, one with the Eternal Word,...
Heart of Jesus, Infinite in Majesty,...
Heart of Jesus, Holy Temple of God,...
Heart of Jesus, Tabernacle of the Most High,...
Heart of Jesus, House of God, and Gate of Heaven,...
Heart of Jesus, aflame with love for us,...
Heart of Jesus, source of justice and love,...
Heart of Jesus, full of goodness and love,...
Heart of Jesus, well-spring of all virtue,...
Heart of Jesus, worthy of all praise,...
Heart of Jesus, King and center of all hearts,...
Heart of Jesus, treasure-house of wisdom and knowledge,...
Heart of Jesus, in whom there dwells the fullness of God,...
Heart of Jesus, in whom the Father is well pleased,...
Heart of Jesus, from whose fullness we have all received,...
Heart of Jesus, desire of the eternal hills,...
Heart of Jesus, patient and full of mercy,...
Heart of Jesus, generous to all who turn to you,...
Heart of Jesus, fountain of life and holiness,...
Heart of Jesus, atonement for our sins,

Heart of Jesus, overwhelmed with insults, **have mercy on us.**
Heart of Jesus, broken for our sins,...
Heart of Jesus, obedient even to death,...
Heart of Jesus, pierced by a lance,...
Heart of Jesus, source of all consolation,...
Heart of Jesus, our life and resurrection,...
Heart of Jesus, our peace and reconciliation,...
Heart of Jesus, victim of our sins,...
Heart of Jesus, salvation of all who trust in You,...
Heart of Jesus, hope of all who die in You,...
Heart of Jesus, delight of all the Saints,...

Lamb of God, you take away the sins of the world, have mercy on us *(3x)*

Jesus, meek and humble of heart. Make our hearts like unto Thine.
Let us pray: Grant, we pray, almighty God, that we, who glory in the Heart of your beloved Son and recall the wonders of his love for us, may be made worthy to receive an overflowing measure of grace from that fount of heavenly gifts. Through Christ our Lord. Amen.

254. Litany of the Precious Blood

Lord, have mercy. Christ, have mercy.
Lord, have mercy. Christ, hear us. Christ, graciously hear us.

God, the Father of Heaven, ... **Have mercy on us.**
God, the Son, Redeemer of the world,...
God, the Holy Spirit,...
Holy Trinity, One God,...
Blood of Christ, only-begotten Son of the Eternal Father, **Save us.**
Blood of Christ, Incarnate Word of God,...
Blood of Christ, of the New and Eternal Testament,...
Blood of Christ, falling upon the earth in the Agony,...
Blood of Christ, shed profusely in the Scourging,...
Blood of Christ, flowing forth in the Crowning with Thorns,...
Blood of Christ, poured out on the Cross,...
Blood of Christ, price of our salvation,...
Blood of Christ, without which there is no forgiveness,...
Blood of Christ, Eucharistic drink and refreshment of souls,...
Blood of Christ, stream of mercy,...
Blood of Christ, victor over demons,...
Blood of Christ, courage of Martyrs,...
Blood of Christ, strength of Confessors,...
Blood of Christ, bringing forth Virgins,...
Blood of Christ, help of those in peril,...
Blood of Christ, relief of the burdened,...
Blood of Christ, solace in sorrow,...
Blood of Christ, hope of the penitent,...
Blood of Christ, consolation of the dying,...
Blood of Christ, peace and tenderness of hearts,...
Blood of Christ, pledge of eternal life,...
Blood of Christ, freeing souls from purgatory,...

Blood of Christ, most worthy of all glory and honor,...

Lamb of God, who takes away the sins of the world, **spare us, O Lord.**
Lamb of God, who takes away the sins of the world, **graciously hear us, O Lord.**
Lamb of God, who takes away the sins of the world, **have mercy on us, O Lord.**

You have redeemed us, O Lord, in your Blood. **And made us, for our God, a kingdom.**

Let us pray, Almighty and Eternal God; You have appointed Your only-begotten Son the Redeemer of the world and willed to be appeased by His Blood. Grant we beg of You, that we may worthily adore this price of our salvation, and through its power be safeguarded from the evils of the present life, so that we may rejoice in its fruits forever in heaven. Through the same Christ our Lord. Amen.

255. Litany of Loreto

Lord, have mercy on us. Christ, have mercy on us.
Lord, have mercy on us. Christ, hear us. Christ, graciously hear us.

God the Father of Heaven, **have mercy on us.**
God the Son, Redeemer of the world,...
God the Holy Spirit,...
Holy Trinity, One God,...

Holy Mary, **pray for us.**
Holy Mother of God,...
Holy Virgin of virgins,...
Mother of Christ,...
Mother of the Church,...
Mother of Mercy,...
Mother of Divine Grace,...
Mother of Hope,...
Mother most pure,...
Mother most chaste,...
Mother inviolate,...
Mother undefiled,...
Mother most amiable,...
Mother admirable,...
Mother of good counsel,...
Mother of our Creator,...
Mother of our Saviour,...
Virgin most prudent,...
Virgin most venerable,...
Virgin most renowned,...
Virgin most powerful,...
Virgin most merciful,...
Virgin most faithful,...

Mirror of justice, **pray for us.**
Seat of wisdom,...
Cause of our joy,...
Spiritual vessel,...
Vessel of honor,...
Singular vessel of devotion,...
Mystical rose,...
Tower of David,...
Tower of Ivory,...
House of gold,...
Ark of the covenant,...
Gate of heaven,...
Morning star,...
Health of the sick,...
Refuge of sinners,...
Solace of Migrants,...
Comfort of the afflicted,...
Help of Christians,...
Queen of Angels,...
Queen of Patriarchs,...
Queen of Prophets,...
Queen of Apostles,...
Queen of Martyrs,...
Queen of Confessors,...
Queen of Virgins,...
Queen of all Saints,...
Queen conceived without original sin,...
Queen assumed into heaven,...
Queen of the most holy Rosary,...
Queen of families,...
Queen of peace,...

Litanies: Litany of Loreto

Lamb of God, who takes away the sins of the world, **spare us, O Lord.**
Lamb of God, who takes away the sins of the world, **graciously hear us, O Lord.**
Lamb of God, who takes away the sins of the world, **have mercy on us.**

Pray for us, O holy Mother of God. **That we may be made worthy of the promises of Christ.**

Let us pray. Grant, we beseech thee, O Lord God, that we, Your servants, may enjoy perpetual health of mind and body, and by the glorious intercession of the Blessed Mary, ever Virgin, may be delivered from present sorrow and obtain eternal joy. Through Christ our Lord. Amen.

256. Litany of the Immaculate Heart of Mary

Lord, have mercy on us. Christ, have mercy on us.
Lord, have mercy on us. Christ, hear us. Christ, graciously hear us.

God the Father of Heaven, **have mercy on us.**
God the Son, Redeemer of the world,...
God the Holy Spirit,...
Holy Trinity, One God,...

Immaculate Heart of Mary, favorite Daughter of God the Father, ***pray for us.***
Immaculate Heart of Mary, Mother of God the Son,...
Immaculate Heart of Mary, Spouse of the Holy Ghost,...
Immaculate Heart of Mary, redeemed in a sublime manner by the merits of thy Son,...
Immaculate Heart of Mary, Mother and Model of the Church,...
Immaculate Heart of Mary, excellent exemplar in faith and charity,...
Immaculate Heart of Mary, who conceived the Word of God in thy heart before thou didst in thy womb,...
Immaculate Heart of Mary, who gave precious Blood to the Son of God in His human nature,...
Immaculate Heart of Mary, conceived free of Original Sin,...
Immaculate Heart of Mary, who embraced God's saving will with a full heart, impeded by no sin,...
Immaculate Heart of Mary, whose sweet soul a sword pierced beneath the Cross,...
Immaculate Heart of Mary, given to us as Mother by Jesus as He hung dying on the Cross,...
Immaculate Heart of Mary, who accepted us as sons, as thou stood beneath the Cross,...
Immaculate Heart of Mary, all pure and holy,...

Immaculate Heart of Mary, exalted by Divine grace above all Angels and men, *pray for us.*
Immaculate Heart of Mary, Mediatrix of grace,...

Lamb of God, Who takest away the sins of the world, *spare us, O Lord.*
Lamb of God, Who takest away the sins of the world, *graciously hear us, O Lord.*
Lamb of God, Who takest away the sins of the world, *have mercy on us.*

Pray for us, O Holy Mother of God.
That we may be made worthy of the promises of Christ.

Let us pray: O Immaculate Heart of Mary, filled with love for all thy children upon earth, pray for us who have recourse to thee. Show to our Heavenly Father the wound in the Heart of Thy Son and, at the same time, offer again the sword that pierced thy Sorrowful and Immaculate Heart, as thou suffered by compassion with thy Divine Son for the redemption of the world. By thy intercession, through the merits of Jesus Christ, bring us to salvation. Amen.

257. Litany of Our Lady

Lord, have mercy on us. Christ, have mercy on us.
Lord, have mercy on us. Christ, hear us. Christ, graciously hear us.

God the Father of Heaven, **have mercy on us.**
God the Son, Redeemer of the world,...
God the Holy Spirit,...
Holy Trinity, One God,...
Holy Mary, ***pray for us***
Immaculate Conception,...
Our Lady, Mother of Divine Grace,...
Our Lady, Mother of Our Redeemer,...
Our Lady, Mother of us All,...
Our Lady, Mother of Perpetual Help,...
Our Lady, Mother of Good Counsel,..
Our Lady of Confidence,...
Our Lady of Akita,...
Our Lady of Africa,...
Our Lady of Abundance,...
Our Lady of All Help,...
Our Lady of All Nations,...
Our Lady of Angels,...
Our Lady of Apparitions,...
Our Lady of Bethlehem,...
Our Lady of Charity,...
Our Lady of Clemency,...
Our Lady of Compassion,...
Our Lady of Conquest,...
Our Lady of Czestachowa,...
Our Lady D'Iron,...
Our Lady of Exile,...
Our Lady of Faith,...
Our Lady of Fatima,...

Litanies: Litany of Our Lady

Our Lady of Fire, **pray for us**
Our Lady of Good Deliverance,...
Our Lady of Good Health,...
Our Lady of Good News,...
Our Lady of Good Remedies,...
Our Lady of Good Success,...
Our Lady of Good Tidings,...
Our Lady of Grace,...
Our Lady of Great Power,...
Our Lady of Guadalupe,...
Our Lady of Guard,...
Our Lady of Guidance,...
Our Lady of the Cupboard/Our Lady of Guam,...
Our Lady of Hope,...
Our Lady of Kibeho,...
Our Lady of Knock,...
Our Lady of La Salette,...
Our Lady of Last Agony,...
Our Lady of Life,...
Our Lady of Light,...
Our Lady of Loreto,...
Our Lady of Lourdes,...
Our Lady of Mercy,...
Our Lady of Miracles,...
Our Lady of Mount Carmel,...
Our Lady of Peace,...
Our Lady of Power,...
Our Lady of Port Louis,...
Our Lady of Prosperity,...
Our Lady of Saftey,...
Our Lady of Sorrows,...
Our Lady of Undoer Knots,...

Litanies: Litany of Our Lady

Our Lady of the Armed Forces, **pray for us**
Our Lady of the Assumption,...
Our Lady of the Fountain,...
Our Lady of the Miraculous Medal,...
Our Lady of the Rosary,...
Our Lady of the Sacred Heart,...
Our Lady of the Snows,...
Our Lady of the Woods,...
Our Lady of Victory,...
Our Lady Refuge of Sinners,...
Our Lady, Star of the Sea,...
Our Lady Queen of Families,...
Our Lady Queen of Peace,...
Our Lady, Queen of All Saints,...

O My Lady, pray for us that we may come to know and love Your Divine Son, Jesus, as you do. Mary, take my heart and make it Thine. Amen.

258. Litany of St. Joseph

Lord, have mercy on us. Christ, have mercy on us.
Lord, have mercy on us. Christ, hear us. Christ, graciously hear us.

God the Father of heaven, **have mercy on us.**
God the Son, Redeemer of the World,...
God the Holy Spirit,...
Holy Trinity, one God,...
Holy Mary, **pray for us.**
St. Joseph,...
Renowned offspring of David,...
Light of Patriarchs,...
Spouse of the Mother of God,...
Guardian of the Redeemer,...
Chaste guardian of the Virgin,...
Foster father of the Son of God,...
Diligent protector of Christ,...
Servant of Christ,...
Minister of Salvation,...
Head of the Holy Family,...
Joseph most just,...
Joseph most chaste,...
Joseph most prudent,...
Joseph most strong,...
Joseph most obedient,...
Joseph most faithful,...
Mirror of patience,...
Lover of poverty,...
Model of workers,...
Glory of family life,...
Guardian of virgins,...

Litanies: Litany of St. Joseph

Pillar of families, ***pray for us.***
Support in difficulties,...
Solace of the wretched,...
Hope of the sick,...
Patron of exiles,...
Patron of the afflicted,...
Patron of the poor,...
Patron of the dying,...
Terror of demons,...
Protector of Holy Church,...
Lamb of God, who takes away the sins of the world, ***spare us, O Lord.***
Lamb of God, who takes away the sins of the world, ***graciously hear us, O Lord.***
Lamb of God, who takes away the sins of the world, ***have mercy on us, O Lord.***

He made him the lord of his household. ***And prince over all his possessions.***

Let us pray: O God, in Your ineffable providence; You were pleased to choose Blessed Joseph to be the spouse of Your Most Holy Mother; grant, we beg You, that we may be worthy to have him for our intercessor in heaven whom on earth we venerate as our Protector: You who live and reign forever and ever.

Saint Joseph, pray for us. Amen.

259. Supplications in honor of St. Joseph's hidden life with Jesus and Mary

St. Joseph, pray that Jesus may come into our souls and sanctify us.

St. Joseph, pray that Jesus may come into our hearts and inspire them with charity.

St. Joseph, pray that Jesus may come into our minds and enlighten them.

St. Joseph, pray that Jesus may guide our wills and strengthen them.

St. Joseph, pray that Jesus may direct our thoughts and purify them.

St. Joseph, pray that Jesus may guide our desires and direct them.

St. Joseph, pray that Jesus may look upon our deeds and extend His blessings.

St. Joseph, pray that Jesus may inflame us with love for Him.

St. Joseph, request for us from Jesus the imitation of your virtues.

St. Joseph, request for us from Jesus true humility of spirit.

St. Joseph, request for us from Jesus meekness of heart.

St. Joseph, request for us from Jesus peace of soul.

St. Joseph, request for us from Jesus a holy fear of the Lord.

St. Joseph, request for us from Jesus a desire for perfection.

St. Joseph, request for us from Jesus a gentleness of heart.

St. Joseph, request for us from Jesus a pure and charitable heart.

St. Joseph, request for us from Jesus the wisdom of faith.

St. Joseph, request for us from Jesus His blessing of perseverance in our good deeds.

St. Joseph, request for us from Jesus the strength to carry our crosses.

St. Joseph, request for us from Jesus a disdain for the material goods of this world.

St. Joseph, request for us from Jesus the grace to always walk on the narrow path toward Heaven.

St. Joseph, request for us from Jesus the grace to avoid all occasions of sin.

St. Joseph, request for us from Jesus a holy desire for eternal bliss.

St. Joseph, request for us from Jesus the grace of final perseverance.

St. Joseph, do not abandon us.

St. Joseph, pray that our hearts may never cease to love you and that our lips may ever praise you.

St. Joseph, for the love you did bear for Jesus, grant that we may learn to love Him.

St. Joseph, graciously accept us as your devoted servants.

St. Joseph, we give ourselves to you; accept our pleas and hear our prayers.

St. Joseph, do not abandon us at the hour of our death.

Jesus, Mary, and Joseph, we give you our hearts and our souls.

260. Litany to St. Joseph for a Dying Person

Lord have mercy on us. Christ have mercy on us.
Lord have mercy on us. Christ hear us, Christ graciously hear us.

God the Father of Heaven, **have mercy on us.**
God the Son Redeemer of the World,...
God the Holy Spirit, ...
Holy Trinity One God,...
Holy Mary, **pray for us.**
St. Joseph foster father of Christ, **we beseech thee to hear us.**
St. Joseph patron of the dying,...
St. Joseph attain for those dying forgiveness of their sins,...
St. Joseph attain for them great patience,...
St. Joseph attain for them perfect resignation, ...
St. Joseph attain for them a living and unshakable faith,...
St. Joseph attain for them a firm confidence,...
St. Joseph attain for them ardent charity,...
Avert from them the attack of the enemy,...
Protect them from temptations that assail them,...
Preserve them from all despondency and despair,...
Obtain for them the grace of Jesus Christ,...
Assist them and do not abandon them,...
Come to their aid in their weakness,...
Assist them in their abandonment,...
Attain for them a happy death,...
Obtain for them a merciful judgment,...
Conduct their souls to the vision of Jesus, There to obtain mercy for them Amen.
O Good St. Joseph pray for us! Intercede for us!

261. Litany of Spiritual Warfare
part 3*

O Lord Jesus Christ, *keep us free from the snares of the Evil One.*

By the strength of Your most holy Incarnation,
   free us from evil, Lord Jesus!
By the strength of Your mysterious hidden life,...
By the strength of Your life-giving Baptism,...
By the strength of Your holy miracles,...
By the strength of your good and mighty deeds,...
By the strength of Your preaching of the Gospel,...
By the strength of Your most luminous Transfiguration,...
By the strength of the institution of Your holy Church,...
By the strength of Your institution of the Most Holy Eucharist, by the strength of Your redeeming Passion,...
By the strength of Your saving Crucifixion,...
By the strength *(bow)* of Your most solemn Death,...
By the strength of Your most glorious Resurrection,...
By the strength of Your most blessed Ascension,...
By the strength of Your sending of the Holy Spirit,...
By the strength of the preaching of Your holy Apostles,...
By the strength of the good and mighty deeds of Your holy Apostles,...
By the strength of the faith of Your holy Church,...
By the strength of the good works of Your holy Church,...
By the strength of the sacraments of Your holy Church,...
By the strength of all the Holy Masses of Your holy Church,...
By the strength of the intercession of all Your Saints and Angels,...

Almighty and Ever-living God, through Jesus Christ, Your Son,

Litanies: Litany of Spiritual Warfare

You offer to us the fullness of life in this world and the joy of eternal life forever in Your Kingdom. Through the merits of Jesus Christ, our Lord, and Savior, and by the intercession of Mary, the Mother of God, and of all the Saints and Angels, may we know Your protection in this life from all the snares of the Devil. Help us to remain faithful to You so that we may enjoy the glory of heaven in the life to come. Be always near us, protect us from all evil, grant us Your blessings, clothe us with the full Armor of God, and grant us continued strength and grace in our earthly battle against Satan and all the powers of darkness.

We ask this in the name of Jesus Christ, Your Son, who lives and reigns with You and the Holy Spirit, one God, forever and ever.

*This litany is very long. Only a portion has been used for the Rosary Family Prayer sessions.

262. Litany of the Saints

Lord, have mercy on us. Christ, have mercy on us.
Lord, have mercy on us. Christ, hear us, Christ, graciously hear us.

God, our Heavenly Father, **have mercy on us.**
God the Son, Redeemer of the world,...
God the Holy Spirit,...
Holy Trinity, one God,...
Holy Mary, *pray for us.*
Holy Mother of God,...
Holy Virgin of virgins,...
Saint Michael,...
Saint Gabriel,...
Saint Raphael,...
All you holy Angels and Archangels,...
All you holy orders of blessed Spirits,...
Saint John the Baptist,...
Saint Joseph,...
All you holy Patriarchs and Prophets,...
Saint Peter,...
Saint Paul,...
Saint Andrew,...
Saint James,...
Saint John,...
Saint Thomas,...
Saint James,...
Saint Philip,...
Saint Bartholomew,..
Saint Matthew,...

Saint Simon, ***pray for us.***
Saint Thaddeus,...
Saint Matthias,...
Saint Barnabas,...
Saint Luke,...
Saint Mark,...
All you holy Apostles and Evangelists,...
All you holy Disciples of the Lord,...
All you holy Innocents,...
Saint Stephen,...
Saint Lawrence,...
Saint Vincent,...
Saint Fabian and Saint Sebastian,...
Saint John and Saint Paul,...
Saint Cosmas and Saint Damian,...
Saint Gervase and Saint Protase,...
All you holy Martyrs,...
Saint Silvester,...
Saint Gregory,...
Saint Ambrose,...
Saint Augustine,...
Saint Jerome,...
Saint Martin,...
Saint Nicholas,...
All you holy Bishops and Confessors,...
All you holy Doctors,...
Saint Anthony,...
Saint Benedict,...
Saint Bernard,...
Saint Dominic,...
Saint Francis,...
All you holy Priests and Clergy,...

All you holy Monks and Hermits, **pray for us.**
Saint Mary Magdalene,...
Saint Agatha,...
Saint Lucy,...
Saint Agnes,...
Saint Cecilia,...
Saint Catharine,...
Saint Anastasia,...
All you holy Virgins and Widows,...
All you Saints of God,...
 Lord be merciful, **Lord, save Your people.**
From every evil,...
From every sin,...
From Your anger,...
From sudden and unforeseen death,...
From the snares of the devil,...
From anger, hatred, and ill will,...
From the spirit of uncleanness,...
From lightning and tempest,...
From the scourge of earthquake,...
From plague, famine, and war,...
From everlasting death,...
By the mystery of Your Holy Incarnation,...
By Your Coming,...
By Your Birth,...
By Your Baptism and Holy Fasting,...
By Your Cross and suffering,...
By Your Death and Burial,...
By Your Holy Resurrection,...
By Your wonderful Ascension,...
By the coming of the Holy Spirit, the Paraclete,...
On the day of Judgment,...

Litanies: Litany of the Saints

Be merciful to us sinners, **Lord, hear our prayer.**
That You will spare us,...
That You will pardon us,...
That it may please You to bring us to true repentance,...
To govern and preserve Your holy Church,...
To preserve in holy religion the Pope, and all Holy Orders,...
To humble the enemies of Holy Church,...
To give peace and unity to the whole Christian people,...
To recall to the unity of the Church all those who are straying, to bring all unbelievers to the light of the Gospel,...
To strengthen and preserve us in Your holy service,...
To raise our minds to desire the things of heaven,...
To reward all our benefactors with eternal blessings,...
To deliver our souls from eternal damnation, and the souls of our brethren, kinsmen, and benefactors,...
To give and preserve the fruits of the earth,...
To grant eternal rest to all the faithful departed, That it may please You to hear and heed us, Jesus, Son of the living God,...

Lamb of God, who takes away the sins of the world, **spare us, O Lord.**
Lamb of God, who takes away the sins of the world, **graciously hear us, O Lord.**
Lamb of God, who takes away the sins of the world, **have mercy on us.**

Christ, hear us. **Christ, graciously hear us.**
Lord Jesus, hear our prayer. **Lord Jesus, hear our prayer.**
Lord, have mercy. **Lord, have mercy.**
Christ, have mercy. **Christ, have mercy.**
Lord, have mercy. **Lord, have mercy.**
Amen.

263. Litany of the Holy Angels

Lord, have mercy. Christ have mercy.
Lord, have mercy. Christ hear us. Christ, graciously hear us.

God the Father , Creator of Angels, **have mercy on us.**
God the Son, Lord of Angels,...
God the Holy Spirit, Life of Angels,...
Holy Trinity, Delight of Angels,...
Holy Mary, Queen of Angels, **pray for us.**
All you Choirs of Blessed Spirits,...
Holy Seraphim, Angels of the Lord,...
Holy Cherubim, Angels of the Word,...
Holy Thrones, Angels fo Life,...
Holy Angels, of Adoration, ...
Holy Domination,...
Holy Powers,...
Holy Principalities,...
Holy Virtues,...
Holy Archangel Michael,...
Holy Michael, Conqueror of lucifier,...
Holy Michael, Angel of faith and humility,...
Holy Michael, Guardian of the Anointing of the Sick,...
Holy Michael, Patron of the dying,...
Holy Michael, Prince of the Heavenly Hosts,...
Holy Michael, guide of souls to the Judgement Seat of God,...
Holy Archangel Gabriel,...
Holy Gabriel, Agnel of the Incarnation,...
Holy Gabriel, Faithful Messenger of God,...
Holy Angel, of hope and peace,...
Holy Gabriel, Protector of all Servants and Handmaids of God,...

Litanies: Litany of the Holy Angels

Holy Gabriel, Guardian of Baptism, ***pray for us.***
Holy Gabriel, Patron of Priests,...
Holy Archangel Raphael,...
Holy Raphael, Angel of Divine Love,...
Holy Raphael, Conqueror of the hellish fiend,...
Holy Raphael, Helper in Great Distress,...
Angel of suffering and healing,...
Holy Raphael, Patron of Physicians, Wanderers, and Travelers,...
All you Holy Archangels,...
Holy Archangels, Angels of Service before the Throne of God,...
Holy Archangels, Angels of Service for Mankind,...
Holy Guardian Angels, pray for us,...
Guardian Angels, Helper in all of our needs,...
Holy Angels, Light in all darkness,...
Guardian Angels, support in all danger,...
Guardian Angels, admonishers of our consciences,...
Guardian Angels, intecessors before the Throne of God,...
Guardian Angels, shield and defense against evil spirits,...
Guardian Angels, our constant companions,...
Guardian Angels, our safest guides,...
Guardian Angels, our truest friends,...
Guardian Angels, our wisest counselors,...
Guardian Angels, our models of prompt obedience,...
Guardian Angels, comforter in abandonment,...
Guardian Angels, mirrors of humility and sincerity,...
Guardian Angels, Angels of our families,...
Guardian Angels, Angels of our priest and pastors,...
Guardian Angels of our children,...
Guardian Angels of our homes and country,...
Guardian Angels, of Holy Mother, the Church,...
All you Holy Angels,...
During life, ***assist us.***

Litanies: Litany of the Holy Angels

In death, assist us.

In Heaven, we shall be grateful to you.

Lamb of God, Who takest away the sins of the world, **spare us, O Lord.**

Lamb of God, Who takest away the sins of the world, **graciously hear us, O Lord.**

Lamb of God, Who takest away the sins of the world, **have mercy on us.**

Christ hear us, **Christ graciously hear us.**

God has given his Angels charge over you, to guard you in all your ways.

Let us pray. Almighty Eternal God, grant us the help of Your heavenly Hosts that that we may be preserved from the terrible souls of the evil one by the Precious Blood of our Lord, Jesus Christ, and the intercession of the Most Blessed Immaculate Virgin Mary; so that free from all adversity we may serve You again in peace through Christ our Lord. Amen.

264. Supplication of the Holy Angels

Almighty, Eternal Triune God, before we implore Your servants, the Holy Angels, and call upon them for help, we fall on our knees and adore You, Father, Son, and Holy Spirit (+). Be honored and praised for all eternity, and may all angels and men, whom You created, adore, love, and serve You, O Holy, Mighty, and Immortal God! You also, Mary, Queen of the Angels, graciously accept the supplications we address to your servants. We beg you, Mediatrix of all Graces and all-powerful Intercessor, bring these our petitions to the throne of the Most High that we may find grace, salvation, and help! Amen. You great, Holy Angels, you have been given to us by God for our protection and help!

We implore you in the name of the Triune God: ***hasten to help us!***
We implore you in the name of the Precious Blood of Our Lord Jesus Christ:
We implore you in the all-powerful name of Jesus:
We implore you by all the wounds of Our Lord Jesus:
We implore you by all the sufferings of Our Lord Jesus:
We implore you by the holy word of God:
We implore you by the Heart of Our Lord Jesus:
We implore you in the name of God's love for us, the poor:
We implore you in the name of God's faithfulness to us, the poor:
We implore you in the name of God's mercy toward us, the poor:
We implore you in the name of Mary, Queen of Heaven and earth:
We implore you in the name of Mary, your Queen and Lady:
We implore you by your own beatitude:
We implore you by your own fidelity:
We implore you by your warfare for the kingdom of God:
We implore you: Cover us with your shield!
We implore you: Protect us with your sword!

We implore you: Illumine us with your light!
We implore you: Save us under the protective mantel of Mary!
We implore you: Hide us in the heart of Mary!
We implore you: Place us in the hands of Mary!
We implore you: Show us the way to the gate of life, the open Heart of Our Lord!
We implore you: Guide us safely to the heavenly Father's House!
All you nine choirs of blessed spirits, hasten to help us!
You, our special companions, who have been given to us by God, hasten to help us!
Hasten to help us, we implore you!

The Precious Blood of Our Lord and King was poured out for the sake of us, the poor: **hasten, help us, we implore you!**
The Heart of Our Lord and King beats in love of us, the poor:
The Immaculate Heart of Mary, most pure, Your Queen, beats in love for us, the poor:

St. Michael, the Archangel, Prince of the heavenly hosts, conqueror of the infernal dragon, you received from God the strength and power to destroy with humility the pride of the powers of darkness. We implore you help us to true humility of heart, to unshakable fidelity to fulfill always the Will of God, and to fortitude in sufferings and trials. Help us to stand before the judgment seat of God!

St. Gabriel, the Archangel, Angel of the Incarnation, faithful messenger of God, open our ears to even the gentle warnings and appeals of the loving Heart of Our Lord. Stand ever before us, we implore you that we may properly understand the Word of God, follow and obey it, and fulfill that which God expects of us. Help us to be watchful readiness so that when the Lord comes, He may not find us sleeping!

St. Raphael, the Archangel, arrow, and medicine of Divine love, wound our hearts; we implore you, with the burning love of God and, let this wound never heal so that even in daily life, we might always remain upon the path of love and overcome all things through love!

Help us great and holy brothers, fellow servants before God!

Protect us from ourselves, from our own cowardice and tepidity, from our self-seeking and avarice, from our envy and mistrust, from our craving for satiation, comfort, and recognition. Free us from the bonds of sin and attachment to worldly things. Take the blindfold from our eyes that we ourselves placed there so that we might not see the misery around us but complacently look to and pity ourselves. Set the goad of holy restlessness for God in our hearts so that we never cease to seek God with longing, contrition, and love!

Behold, the Precious Blood of Our Lord which was shed for our sake. Behold the tears of your Queen, which she shed for our sake. Behold the Divine Image in us, which God so lovingly impressed upon our souls and which is now disfigured by our sins. Help us to know and adore God, to love and serve Him! Help us in the battle with the powers of darkness, who insidiously stalk and oppress us! Help us that none of us may be lost, but rather rejoicing, we may one day be united in eternal happiness! Amen.

265. Litany of St. Michael, the Archangel

Lord, have mercy. Christ, have mercy.
Lord, have mercy. Christ, hear us. Christ, graciously hear us.

God the Father of heaven, **have mercy on us.**
God the Son, Redeemer of the world,...
God the Holy Spirit,...
Holy Trinity, one God,...
Holy Mary, Queen of Angels, **pray for us.**
Saint Michael,...
Saint Michael, abundant font of divine wisdom,...
Saint Michael, most perfect adorer of the Divine Word,...
Saint Michael, whom God crowned with honor and glory,...
Saint Michael, most powerful Prince of the heavenly host,...
Saint Michael, standard-bearer of the Most Holy Trinity,...
Saint Michael, guardian of Paradise,...
Saint Michael, guide and consoler of the People of God,...
Saint Michael, splendor and fortitude of the Church Militant,...
Saint Michael, honor and joy of the Church Triumphant,...
Saint Michael, light of the Angels,...
Saint Michael, protection of orthodox people,...
Saint Michael, strength of those who fight under the standard of the Cross,...
Saint Michael, light and hope of souls near death,...
Saint Michael, our most sure aid,...
Saint Michael, help in our adversities,...
Saint Michael, herald of the everlasting judgment,...
Saint Michael, consoler of souls languishing in purgatory,...
Saint Michael, receiver of the souls of the elect after death,...
Saint Michael, our prince,...
Saint Michael, our defender,...

Litanies: Litany of the St. Michael

Lamb of God, who takest away the sins of the world, **spare us, O Lord.**

Lamb of God, who takest away the sins of the world, **graciously hear us, O Lord.**

Lamb of God, who takest away the sins of the world, **have mercy on us.**

Pray for us, Saint Michael the Archangel, **that we may be made worthy of the promises of Christ.**

Let us pray. O Lord Jesus Christ, may Your continual blessing sanctify us and grant us through the intercession of Saint Michael the wisdom that teaches us to lay up our treasure in Heaven and choose eternal goods over those of this world. Thou, who lives and reigns forever. Amen

266. Litany for the Holy Souls in Purgatory

For my dear parents and grandparents, **Jesus, have mercy!**
My brothers and sisters and other near relatives,...
My godparents and sponsors of confirmation,...
My spiritual and temporal benefactors,...
My friends and neighbors,...
All for whom love or duty calls me to pray,...
Those who have suffered disadvantages or harm through me,...
Those who are especially beloved by you,...
Those whose release is near at hand,...
Those who desire most to be united with you,...
Those who endure the greatest sufferings,...
Those who are least remembered,...
Those whose release is most remote,...
Those who are most deserving because of their services to the Church,...
The rich, who now are the most destitute,...
The mighty, who now are powerless,...
The once spiritually blind, who now see their folly,...
The frivolous, who spent their time in idleness,...
The poor who did not seek the treasures of heaven,...
The tepid, who devoted little time to prayer,...
The indolent, who neglected to perform good works,...
Those of little faith, who neglected the frequent reception of the sacraments,...
The habitual sinners, who owe their salvation to a miracle of grace,...
Parents who failed to watch over their children,...
Superiors who were not solicitous for the salvation of those entrusted to them,...
Those who strove for worldly riches and pleasures,...
The worldly-minded, who failed to use their wealth and talents in the service of God,...

Those who witnessed the death of others but would not think of their own, ***Jesus, have mercy!***
Those who did not provide for the life hereafter,...
Those whose sentence is severe because of the great things entrusted to them,...
The popes, kings, and rulers,...
The bishops and their counselors,...
My teachers and spiritual advisers,...
The priests and religious of the Catholic Church,...
The defenders of the holy faith,...
Those who died on the battlefield,...
Those who fought for their country,...
Those who were buried in the sea,...
Those who died of strokes,...
Those who died of heart attacks,...
Those who suffered and died of cancer or AIDS,...
Those who died suddenly in accidents,...
Those who died without the last rites of the Church,...
Those who shall die within the next 24 hours,...
For my own poor soul when I shall have to appear before your judgment seat,...

Eternal rest grant unto them, O Lord. Let perpetual light shine upon them forever more with your Saints in heaven because you are so gracious.
The Lord be with you. ***And with your Spirit.***

May the prayer of Your suppliant people, we beseech You, O Lord, benefit the souls of Your departed servants and handmaids. Deliver them from all their sins and make them partakers of Your redemption. Amen.

267. Litany of Healing for Families

Heavenly Father, I give You thanks, honor, glory, and praise for my family. I ask You, in the Name of Your Son, Jesus, to bless and protect each one of us and help us to be attentive to Your plans for our lives. I also ask You to preserve our health and to heal us individually and collectively as a family unit. To heal us spiritually, emotionally, and physically for Your greater glory. Remove all obstacles, any unforgiveness, negative inner vows we've made, oppressive, ungodly spirits, preventing a harmonious spirit and cooperative behavior within our family.

I believe in You, Lord! Help my unbelief! May Your will be done!

From all habits of sin preventing a close relationship with you, ***heal my family, O Jesus.***
From anything preventing a Spirit-driven life,...
From anything preventing acceptance of the Father-God's unconditional love he has for us as adopted sons and daughters,...
From anything preventing the peace, joy, goodness, and unity that only You can provide,...
From anything preventing having the mustard seed faith that can move mountains,...
From all forms of selfishness and pride,...
From all inherited spiritual defects,...
From spiritual apathy,...
From all forms of sinful addiction,...
From the effects of painful memories,...
From bondage caused by negative inner vows,...
From all the effects of broken relationships due to unforgiveness, adultery, divorce, and the various forms of abuse,...
From all unhealthy attachments,...

Litanies: Litany of Healing for Families

From all ungodly emotions, attitudes, and behaviors, pettiness, manipulation, argumentativeness, jealousy, **heal my family, O Jesus.**
From all inherited emotional and psychological defects,...
From all emotional and psychological illnesses,...
From all inherited physical defects,...
From all physical afflictions and illnesses,...

Lord, increase the virtue of **faith** in my family.
Lord, increase the virtue of **hope** in my family.
Lord, increase the virtue of **charity** in my family.

Help us, O Lord, to internalize the words of Joshua: "As for me and my household, we will serve the Lord." *(Joshua 24:15)*. Amen.

268. Litany of the Dust

For those who have betrayed us...***Father, forgive them.***
For those who have let us down...(Repeat: Father, forgive them.)
For those who have been indifferent to us...
For those who have crippled our lives...
For those who have doubted us...
For those who have accused us...
For those who have preferred others to us...
For family members who have hurt us...
For friends who have denied us...
For those who have walked away from us...
For my own self-pity...
For my lukewarmness...
For my times of despair and distrust...
For my refusals to be hugged...
For my disbelief in your love...
For my searchings everywhere but in your heart...
For apologies frozen on my lips...
For my words of love unspoken...
For my kisses and embraces ungiven...
For compliments never offered...
For a heart closed in self-centeredness...
For my own unforgiving postures...
For not believing in your forgiveness...

O Jesus, you who offered forgiveness to so many to Mary, the Crippled Man, the Good Thief who said that You came to give life and shed Your Blood "for the forgiveness of sins," forgive us our sins. Not only the obvious ones but especially the unnoticed ones of pride, righteousness, self-hate, and the refusal to be loved. Take our very selves and wash them in that unconditional love of Yours, for You are a God of mercy and compassion, You who live and love forever and ever. Amen.

269. Litany of Humility
(Condensed)

Jesus, meek and humble of heart--**Hear me.**

From the desire of being esteemed--**Deliver me, O Jesus.**

From the desire of being loved,...

From the desire of being extolled,...

From the desire of being honored,...

From the desire of being praised,...

From the desire of being preferred to others,...

From the desire of being consulted,...

From the desire of being approved,...

From the fear of being humiliated,...

From the fear of being despised,...

From the fear of suffering rebukes,...

From the fear of being calumniated,...

From the fear of being forgotten,...

From the fear of being ridiculed,...

From the fear of being wronged,...

From the fear of being suspected,...

That others may be loved more than I, **Jesus, grant me the grace to desire it.**

That others may be esteemed more than I,...

That, in the opinion of the world, others may increase, and I may decrease,...

That others may be chosen, and I set aside,...

That others may be praised and I unnoticed,...

That others may be preferred to me in everything,...

That others may become holier than I, provided that I may become as holy as I should,...

O Jesus, meek and humble of Heart, **Make my heart like unto Thine. Amen.**

270. Litany of Waiting
By Sr. Josephine (Condensed)

From the fear of waiting, **deliver me, Jesus.**
From the fear of uncertainty...
From the fear of failure...
From the fear of change...
From the fear that Your promises will not come true...
From the fear that my suffering has no meaning...
From the fear that my suffering will bear no fruit...
From the fear of my weaknesses...
From the fear that Your grace will not be sufficient...
From the fear that Your will is not for my good...
From the fear that Your plans will not fulfill the desires of my heart,...
From the belief that I wait alone,...
From the belief that I am waiting because I have done something wrong...
From the belief that I will wait forever without resolution...
From the belief that I am waiting because You will never respond...
From the belief that You have abandoned me in my waiting...
From the taunt of temptation and discouragement that whisper to me when I am waiting,...
When it is hard to wait joyfully, **Jesus, I will wait with You.**
When my prayers seem unanswered...
When my struggles are overwhelming...
In my joys & in my sorrows...
In the ordinary events of daily life...
In times of celebration...
When I feel stuck...
When discerning big decisions...
When I am tired or sick...
When I am uncertain...
When no one else will wait with me...
Throughout the pilgrimage of my life,...

271. Litany of Thanksgiving
By St. Faustina

Thank You, O God, for all the graces which unceasingly You lavish upon me, graces which enlighten me with the brilliance of the sun, for by them You show me the sure way.

Thank You, O Lord, for creating me, for calling me into being from nothingness, for imprinting Your divinity on my soul, the work of sheer merciful love.

Thank You, O God, for Holy Baptism, which engrafted me into Your family, a gift great beyond all thought or expression which transforms my soul.

Thank You, O Lord, for Holy Confession, for that inexhaustible spring of great mercy, for that inconceivable fountain of graces in which sin-tainted souls become purified.

Thank You, O Jesus, for Holy Communion in which You give us Yourself. I feel Your Heart beating within my breast as You cause Your divine life to unfold within me.

Thank You, O Holy Spirit, for the Sacrament of Confirmation, which dubs me Your knight and gives strength to my soul at each moment, protecting me from evil.

Thank You, O God, for the grace of a vocation. For being called to serve You alone, leading me to make You my sole love, an unequal honor for my soul.

Thank You, O Lord, for perpetual vows, for that union of pure love, for having deigned to unite Your pure heart with mine and uniting my heart to Yours in the purest of bonds.

Thank You, O Lord, for the Sacrament of Anointing, which, in my final moments, will give me strength, my help in battle, my guide to salvation, fortifying my soul till we rejoice forever.

Thank You, O God, for all the inspirations that Your goodness lavishes upon me, for the interior lights given my soul, which the heart senses but words cannot express.

Thank You, O Holy Trinity, for the vastness of the graces which You have lavished on me unceasingly through life. My gratitude will intensify as the eternal dawn rises when, for the first time, I sing to Your glory. Amen.

272. As I Am Lord

Because I am obnoxious, *forgive me, Lord.*
Because I am dishonest,...
Because I am egotistical,...
Because I am undisciplined,...
Because I am weak,...
Because I am impure,...
Because I am arrogant,...
Because I am self-centered,...
Because I am pompous,...
Because I am insincere,...
Because I am unchaste,...
Because I am grasping,...
Because I am judgmental,...
Because I am impatient,...
Because I am shallow,...
Because I am inconsistent,...
Because I am unfaithful,...
Because I am immoral,...
Because I am ungrateful,...
Because I am disobedient,...
Because I am selfish,...
Because I am lukewarm,...
Because I am slothful,...
Because I am unloving,...
Because I am uncommitted,...
Because I am sinful,...

Because I am loved by You, **thank You, Lord!**

Concluding Prayers

Guided Meditation

273.1 Short Surrender Prayer

O Jesus, I surrender myself to You, take care of everything. (10xs)

273.2 Longer Prayer of Surrender

Dear Lord Jesus, it is my will to surrender to You everything that I am and everything that I am striving to be. I open the deepest recesses of my heart and invite Your Holy Spirit to dwell inside of me. I offer You my life, heart, mind, body, soul, spirit, and all my hopes, plans, and dreams. I surrender to You my past, present, and future problems, habits, character defects, attitudes, livelihood, resources, finances, medical coverage, occupation, and all my relationships.

I give You my health, physical appearance, disabilities, family, marriage, children, and friendships. I ask You to take Lordship over every aspect of my life. I surrender to You all my hurt, pain, worry, doubt, fear, and anxiety, and I ask You to wash me clean.

I release everything into Your compassionate care. Please speak to me clearly, Lord. Open my ears to hear Your voice. Open my heart to commune with You more deeply. I want to feel Your loving embrace. Open the doors that need to be opened and close the doors that need to be closed. Please set my feet upon the straight and narrow road that leads to everlasting life with You. Amen

Concluding Prayers

274. Fill in the Gap

These vary depending on the day; below are most commonly used.

O Lord Jesus, fill in the gap between:
- The love I have given others today & the love they needed.
- The love I have given family, relatives, friends, neighbors, co-workers & the love they needed.
- Those I may have hurt in life and the love they needed.
- The love I received from others today and the love I needed.
- The love I received from family, relatives, friends, neighbors, & co-workers & the love I needed.
- Those who have ever hurt me or my loved ones from the love we were given and the love we needed.

Above all, I pray Lord Jesus fill in the huge gap, between the love I have given the Heavenly Father I the love He should have received from me, His child.

275. Fill in the Gap for deceased loved ones.

Lord, I give *(mention here)* back to You. They belong to You more than to me. But this leaves me with a big void in my heart. Lord, fill that void with Your presence. Fill that void with Your love. Jesus fill in the gaps in my heart with Your love, with Your presence. Make me whole. Amen.

Concluding Prayers

276. Short Prayers

Heavenly Father, please Father me now. (repeat)

Oh Mary, my mother, be my mother now. (repeat)

277. Prayer for Daily Neglects

Eternal Father, I offer Thee the Sacred Heart of Jesus, with all its love, all its sufferings and all its merits.

First --- To expiate all the sins I have committed this day and during all my life. *Glory Be...*

Second --- To purify the good I have done poorly this day and during all my life. *Glory Be...*

Third --- To supply for the good I ought to have done and that I have neglected this day and all my life. *Glory Be...*

278. A Night Prayer

Eternal Father, I desire to rest in Thy Heart this night. I make the intention of offering to Thee every beat of my heart, joining to them as many acts of love and desire. I pray that even while I am asleep, I will bring back to Thee should that offend Thee. I ask forgiveness for the whole world, especially for those who know Thee and yet sin. I offer to Thee my every breath and heartbeat as a prayer of reparation. Amen.

279. Healing Night Prayer

O Come Holy Spirit. Lord, Jesus Christ, through the Power of the Holy Spirit, please go back into my memory as I sleep tonight. Every hurt that's ever been done to me heal that hurt. Every hurt that I've ever caused another person heal that hurt. All the relationships that have been damaged throughout my whole life that I'm not aware of heal those relationships. I choose to forgive, and I ask to be forgiven. Remove whatever bitterness may be in my heart, and Lord, fill the empty spaces with Your Love. Amen.

Concluding Prayers

280. Examination of Blessings

As we come to the close of this day, let's call to mind the blessings, gifts, and graces that were bestowed upon us today. At the same time, we also ask God to show us those "God Moments" or "God-incidences" (*that we don't call them coincidences but "God-incidences"*). We ask God to help us, Come Holy Spirit, help us to see the blessings of this day.

O Come Holy Spirit, Beloved of my soul. Holy Spirit, enlighten my mind, refresh my memory, and help me to see the gifts, the graces, the blessings, and the "God-Moments" of today.

Lord, We thank you for the gifts of:
- Receiving Holy Communion
- Our faith, the gift of the sacraments,
- For friends of faith
- For people we have come into contact with today
- For conversations about our faith
- For the beautiful nature around us
- For family, friendships, happy memories
- For the gift of the rosary and YouTube to pray together
- For the food we have, the roof over our heads or beds to rest
- For the daily discipline of prayer
- For the things on our to-do list that we were able to get done
- For all the unexcepted blessings
- For our senses- smell, taste, see, hear and touch
- For our Guardian Angels and Saints- who lead us, inspire us, guide us, and help us in our prayers and to seek heaven.
- For those who have shown us kindness today in any way

Concluding Prayers
281. Examination of Conscience
*Subject to change daily; below is a brief personal reflection.

Thank you, Jesus. O Come Holy Spirit, help us have humble, contrite hearts. Help us to see and to recognize our sins, our faults, and the failing of this day.

- Did we begin with a firm foundation- offering up the day to the Lord through our Lady?
- Did we practice the heroic minute, to try to mortify ourselves today?
- Did we verify our curiosity?
- Gluttony in regards to food and drink? Mortification and custody of the senses?
- Maybe some special sacrifice God was calling us to today- maybe to keep our mouth shut and not to say something or complain about something?
- Was I faithful today to my daily prayer devotion and commitment to prayer time? Did I witness Christ by blessing myself before and after meals?
- Did I strive to combine every fully deliberate action or at least a moment here with a prayer for Divine Assistance, such as when we're driving?
- Did I take the opportunity to bless ourselves when beginning a new task or driving past a church?
- Was my work done today with excellence? Was my work done in love of doing it for Jesus?
- Was I generous? Did I strive to be cheerful in my dealings?
- How did I use the gift of time God granted me today?
- How often did I get into laziness?
- How often did I make myself the center of attention, either through self-pity, moodiness, anxiety, complaining, critical spirit, or impatience? Bothersome of pride, coveting, lust, anger, gluttony, envy, sloth?
- Did we fall short today of loving with our whole hearts?

Night Prayer

Liturgy of the Hours

These prayers change each day. Below is the basic format. Liturgy of the Hours can be found online, or a breviary can be purchased.

God, come to my assistance.
— Lord, make haste to help me.
Glory Be...

Examination of Blessings/ Examination of Conscience

On pages 224 & 225 is a variation of these examinations. They are not exact, as they change from day to day.

282. Penitential Act

I confess to Almighty God, and to you, my brothers and sisters, that I have greatly sinned through my thoughts and in my words, in what I have done, and in what I have failed to do; through my fault, through my fault, through my most grievous fault; therefore I ask blessed Mary ever-Virgin, all the Angels and Saints, and you, my brothers and sisters, to pray for me to the Lord our God. Amen.

First Psalm

Second Psalm

Scripture

Responsory

Gospel

Concluding Prayer

Blessing

May the All-Powerful Lord grant us a restful night and a peaceful death.

283. Salve Regina

Salve, Regina, Mater misericordiae, vita, dulcedo, et spes nostra, salve. ad te clamamus exsules filii Evae, ad te suspiramus, gementes et flentes in hac lacrimarum valle. Eia, ergo, advocata nostra, illos tuos misericordes oculos ad nos converte; et Iesum, benedictum fructum ventris tui, nobis post hoc exsilium ostende. O clemens, O pia, O dulcis Virgo Maria.

Final Song:

Thank You Jesus, thank You Jesus (*repeat*)

284. Night Blessing for a Good Sleep

In Jesus' (+) Name, I cover myself and all my property with the Blood of Jesus. I take authority over all demons of the night, bad dreams, nightmares, and lascivious dreams, and anyone or anything trying to get into my dreams, and I command them to stay away. I ask for God's holy and powerful Angels to protect me, my property, and all my loved ones as I sleep through the night and the day. I ask for a fiery wall of protection of the Lord around me. Amen.

285. Final Blessing

"We are the Rosary Family; we pray with each other and for each other. Heaven is our home; we are just passing through, and I pray in the Precious Name of Our Lord, Jesus Christ, through the intercession of Mary, that each and every one of us, one day, may be in the Kingdom of Heaven to sing the praise of God for all eternity."

Deceased Loved Ones

Priest & Religious

Prayer Intentions

Prayer Intentions

Prayer Intentions

Prayer Intentions

Prayer Intentions

Prayer Intentions

www.littlewayspublishing.com

Follow Us on Social Media:

Books (Amazon):

Snuggletime Prayer Series are traditional prayers as children's books to help pray with young children.

Divine Praises
Our Father

Door to Heaven Series holds an encounter with a different Saint when you open the book.

St. Therese of Lisieux
Guardian Angel (Coming Soon)

Family Products on Etsy

About us:

Little Ways Publishing, LLC was started at the prompting of St. Therese of Lisieux.

Jackie Allor is a wife, mother of 4 beautiful teens, a graduate of Ave Maria (1st class), and a Cancer Survivor. Part of a large devout Catholic Family in the Archdiocese of Detroit, she is excited to provide our faith communities with family books and activities.

www.ingramcontent.com/pod-product-compliance
Lightning Source LLC
Chambersburg PA
CBHW061938220426
43662CB00012B/1947